Special Educational Needs for Newly Qualified Teachers and Teaching Assistants

This completely revised and updated edition addresses the most recent developments in special educational needs. Essential reading for newly qualified teachers and teaching assistants, Rita Cheminais's classic text now relates to current initiatives including *Every Child Matters* (ECM) and using personalised learning approaches. Many aspects vital to effective classroom practice are explored, including:

- the latest Qualified Teacher Status Standards and the Occupational Standards for Supporting Teaching and Learning in Schools;
- recent legislation and key official reports and documents relating to SEN and *ECM*;
- effective partnership working with multi-agency practitioners;
- up-to-date tips on how to meet Ofsted's inspection requirements in relation to pupils' well-being, attainment and achievement;
- how to evaluate the impact of SEN/additional provision.

The book reflects the DCSF/National Strategies Inclusion Development Programme (IDP), and practical tips and strategies are given on how to meet the needs of a diverse range of pupils with additional educational needs (AEN), including: speech, language and communication needs; moderate learning difficulties; social, emotional and behavioural difficulties; sensory impairments and physical disabilities.

Featuring helpful checklists, templates and photocopiable resources to support professional development, this practical resource contains a wealth of valuable advice, as well as signposting to further information.

This authoritative text will provide fascinating reading for trainee and newly qualified teachers as well as experienced teachers and teaching assistants. Lecturers in higher education and consultants and advisers in Local Authority Children's Services will also find this book a useful resource.

Rita Cheminais is a School Improvement Partner and a freelance education consultant.

Special Educational Needs for Newly Qualified Teachers and Teaching Assistants

A practical guide

Second edition

Rita Cheminais

Routledge
Taylor & Francis Group

LONDON AND NEW YORK

First published 2000
by David Fulton Publishers

This edition published 2010
by Routledge
2 Park Square, Milton Park, Abingdon, Oxon OX14 4RN

Simultaneously published in the USA and Canada
by Routledge
270 Madison Ave, New York, NY 10016

Routledge is an imprint of the Taylor & Francis Group, an informa business

© 2010 Rita Cheminais

Typeset in Bembo by
Keystroke, Tettenhall, Wolverhampton
Printed and bound in Great Britain by
MPG Books Group, UK

British Library Cataloguing in Publication Data
A catalogue record for this book is available from the British Library

Library of Congress Cataloging in Publication Data
Cheminais, Rita.
 Special educational needs for newly qualified teachers and teaching assistants:
 a practical guide/Rita Cheminais. – 2nd ed.
   p. cm.
 Rev. ed. of: Special educational needs for newly qualified and student teachers.
   Includes bibliographical references and index.
 1. Special education–Great Britain. 2. Children with mental disabilities–Education–Great
 Britain. 3. First year teachers–Great Britain. 4. Teachers' assistants–Great Britain.
 I. Cheminais, Rita. Special educational needs for newly qualified and student teachers.
 II. Title.
 LC3986.G7C47 2009
 371.90941–dc22   2009010623

ISBN 10: 0–415–49583–0 (pbk)
ISBN 10: 0–203–87057–3 (ebk)

ISBN 13: 978–0–415–49583–7 (pbk)
ISBN 13: 978–0–203–87057–0 (ebk)

Contents

Illustrations

Figures

Tables

Foreword

This second edition of *Special Educational Needs for Newly Qualified Teachers and Teaching Assistants* helps to put inclusion back into teaching, into schools. Once the buzz word of everything to do with meeting the special educational needs of children in schools, the inclusion agenda has become subsumed within *Every Child Matters*, the overarching agenda for all children and for everyone working with them whether in schools or services. Whilst there are positive aspects of this, there are also some dangers. What is to be welcomed is that the focus is now on the needs of all children and young people, and on a range of needs not just educational. However, the colossal movements involved in bringing about Local Authority integration of services and putting into place complex structural changes means that the system is likely to give less attention to special needs. What this fully revised guide brings, is a wealth of useful information and ideas to assist staff in schools in making inclusion happen. The information is comprehensive and easily found and is likely to support teachers, SENCOs, teaching assistants and other staff training them or working with them.

How does this updated guide assist teaching staff in facilitating inclusion? The demystification of terms and of legislation in Chapter 1 and the practical ideas for teaching and assessment in Chapters 2 and 3 respectively make it more likely that special needs will come within the usual and expected aspects of teaching. Teaching approaches suggested for children with special needs are no different from good teaching approaches for all children. The ideas in this book are therefore relevant to the whole classroom. The guide gives, for example, information on what to do if a child discloses a child protection issue, ways to think about and respond to different aspects of unwanted behaviour, how to develop a personalised learning approach and strategies for developing self esteem. Given the demands on schools, teachers are more likely to feel able to respond to all pupils if information they need is readily available. There are dangers in our current teaching culture in which some children are submitted to a social process, through some critical decisions, that leads to labels including that of 'special needs'. One potential hazard of this is that such labels can allow the removal of responsibility. Systemic avoidance of responsibility can assign children to the gaze of others; in other words to further processes of assessment and classification that may not be necessary. By demystifying teaching for special educational needs, this guide makes it less likely that this will happen.

The training of teachers and teaching assistants is, like education as a whole, a more political landscape than ever before. Consequently, the demands placed on training providers has led some to a lack of attention to issues of inclusive education. As a separate topic, 'special educational needs' is sometimes given less of a focus. However, by seeing inclusion as relevant for all, for some providers this is a lever for putting 'inclusion' at the centre of teacher training and development, as is the case in Aberdeen University, or to make 'inquiry', as an approach that engages all learners in learning, a key tenet of training as is the case in Newcastle University. These initiatives are developing a very different approach to inclusion in its widest sense. This guide facilitates and is complementary to such developments. It helps answer particular questions about, for example, how 'special needs' is different to 'disability', and what are CAF and RAISEonline, and what do different legislative responsibilities for children with disabilities mean for schools? If teachers and teaching assistants have ready answers to such questions, and many more, this is likely to help enormously in enabling them to be free to respond to other initiates.

It has become a potentially unhelpful cliché to underline the importance of partnership between children and young people, parents and a range of teaching and other professionals in meeting the special educational needs of pupils. This is partly because 'partnership' can disempower by co-opting parents and children into a professional view-point if professionals are not sensitive to the ways their assumptions and practices can unwittingly silence the voices of others. The use of the term 'partnership' doesn't adequately represent the complex reality of relationships parents and children, and indeed, professions, are likely to experience. However, the clear and accessible approach of *Special Educational Needs for Newly Qualified Teachers and Teaching Assistants* gives many useful lists, in Chapter 4, to guide a range of interactions. The focus on listening is central, and many of the other suggestions are likely to help a more considered approach to inter-professional relations and to interactions with parents and children.

Children have for too long been the 'absent special guest' (Todd, 2007) in the teaching and assessment of special educational needs – and indeed, one could suggest, in *any* planning of teaching and assessment. There is an array of different ways that this is being challenged, whether by: the direct involvement of children in the introduction of assessment for learning; enquiry based approaches that see children taking more control of their own learning; or school councils and parliaments that make a difference. The direct involvement of children and young people in their learning is a quiet assumption in this Guide, and one that surfaces directly in Chapter 2 on approaches to teaching, in children reflecting on their own learning and in Chapter 3 in involving children and young people in their own assessment.

Liz Todd
Reader in Educational Psychology
School of Education, Communication and Language Sciences
University of Newcastle

References

Black-Hawkins, K., Florian, L. and Martyn Rouse, M. (2007), *Achievement and Inclusion in Schools*. London: Routledge.

Todd, L. (2007) *Partnerships for Inclusive Education: A Critical Approach to Collaborative Working*. London: Routledge.

Acknowledgements

Thanks are due to Alison Foyle, my editor at Routledge/David Fulton Education for encouraging me to write this second completely revised and updated edition of the very first book I ever wrote.

I also wish to thank QCA, the DCSF and Ofsted for granting permission to make reference to some of their materials relating to the *Every Child Matters* outcomes.

Special thanks also go to: Philip Eastwood, SENCO and AST for Initial Teacher Training at St Mary's and St Paul's CE Primary School in Knowsley, for his advice on what trainee and newly qualified teachers and teaching assistants really value in relation to special educational needs, disability, inclusion and *Every Child Matters* practice, knowledge and skills in order to meet the professional and occupational requirements of a children's workforce in the twenty-first century; all the professionals from higher education institutions, local authorities and educational publishing who have promoted and referred to my work in the aspects covered in this revised edition; Lucy Wainwright, acting assistant editor at Routledge/David Fulton Education, and all those who have helped to make this book a reality; last but not least, to my late mother for listening to my ideas regarding the complete revision of this essential book during her last couple of months in the nursing home.

Abbreviations

ADD	attention deficit disorder
ADHD	attention deficit hyperactivity disorder
AEN	additional educational needs
AfL	assessment for learning
ALS	additional literacy support
APP	assessing pupil progress
APS	average point score
ASD	autistic spectrum disorder
AST	Advanced Skills Teacher
BECTA	British Educational Communications and Technology Agency
BESD	behavioural, emotional and social difficulties
BEST	Behaviour Education Support Team
CAF	Common Assessment Framework
CAMHS	Child and Adolescent Mental Health Services
CPD	continuing professional development
CRB	Criminal Records Bureau
CVA	contextual value added
CWDC	Children's Workforce Development Council
CYP	children and young people
DAS	disability access scheme
DCSF	Department for Children, Schools and Families
DDA	Disability Discrimination Act
DED	disability equality duty
DfEE	Department for Education and Employment
DfES	Department for Education and Skills
DH	Department of Health
DME	dual or multiple exceptionalities
DRC	Disability Rights Commission
DVD	digital versatile disc
EAL	English as an additional language
EBD	emotional and behavioural difficulties
ECM	*Every Child Matters*
ELS	early literacy support
EP	educational psychologist

EWO	education welfare officer
EYFS	early years foundation stage
FE	further education
FLS	further literacy support
FSM	free school meals
GEP	group education plan
GP	general practitioner
GSCC	General Social Care Council
GTC	General Teaching Council for England
HI	hearing impairment
HIV	human immunodeficiency virus
HMI	Her Majesty's Inspector
ICT	information communication technology
IDP	Inclusion Development Programme
IEP	individual education plan
ITE	initial teacher education
ITT	initial teacher training
LA	local authority
LAC	looked after child/children
LDD	learning difficulties and/or disabilities
LEA	local education authority
LMS	local management of schools
LP	lead professional
LSA	learning support assistant
MLD	moderate learning difficulties
MS	multiple sclerosis
MSI	multi-sensory impairment
NASUWT	National Association of Schoolmasters Union of Women Teachers
NC	National Curriculum
NCSL	National College for School Leadership
NMC	Nursing and Midwifery Council
NOS	National Occupational Standards
NQT	newly qualified teacher
NSF	National Service Framework
NVQ	National Vocational Qualification
ODD	oppositional defiance disorder
Ofsted	Office for Standards in Education, Children's Services and Skills
PD	physical disability
PE	physical education
PMLD	profound and multiple learning difficulty
PRU	pupil referral unit
PSD	personal and social development
PSHE	personal, social and health education
QCA	Qualifications and Curriculum Authority
QFT	quality-first teaching

QTS	Qualified Teacher Status
RAISE	Reporting and Analysis for Improvement through School Self-Evaluation
RBA	removing barriers to achievement
RE	religious education
SA	school action
SA+	school action plus
SAT	standard assessment task/test
SEAL	social and emotional aspects of learning
SEBS	social, emotional and behavioural skills
SEF	self-evaluation form
SEN	special educational needs
SENCO	special educational needs co-ordinator
SEND	special educational needs and disability
SENDA	Special Educational Needs and Disability Act
SENDIST	Special Educational Needs and Disability Tribunal
SIP	school improvement partner
SLCN	speech, language and communication needs
SLD	severe learning difficulties
SpLD	specific learning difficulties
SSA	special support assistant
TA	teaching assistant
TAC	team around the child
TDA	Training and Development Agency for Schools
TTRB	Teacher Training Resource Bank
UNCRC	United Nations Convention on the Rights of the Child
VAK	visual, auditory, kinaesthetic
VI	visual impairment
WRNA	Workforce Remodelling National Agreement

How to use this book

This book is intended to help trainee and newly qualified teachers (NQTs) and teaching assistants (TAs) working in a range of educational settings such as children's centres, early years settings, primary, secondary and special schools, academies and pupil referral units (PRUs) to implement the government's special educational needs (SEN) and disability frameworks and meet the requirements of the *Every Child Matters* (*ECM*) strategy, as well as the personalised learning and inclusion agendas. The book is also appropriate for all those professionals responsible for contributing to trainee and newly qualified teachers' and teaching assistants' continuing professional development in relation to SEN, disability and *ECM*, for example: SEN co-ordinators (SENCOs), induction tutors and mentors for NQTs and TAs new to the role in supporting and working with pupils with SEN and learning difficulties and disabilities (LDD); local authority consultants, advisers and educational psychologists responsible for delivering training to NQTs and TAs, as well as senior lecturers in the field, providing training for initial teacher training, NQTs and TAs.

The book will enable trainee and newly qualified teachers and teaching assistants to know how to:

- meet the legal requirements and government expectations in relation to SEN, disability, inclusion and *ECM*;

- identify barriers to learning and participation, and which personalised learning approaches to utilise to meet the needs of pupils with SEN/LDD;

- manage, monitor and evaluate provision and practice for pupils with SEN/LDD in order to demonstrate the impact of their interventions on improving outcomes for pupils;

- meet the latest Ofsted inspection requirements;

- work collaboratively with other practitioners to address the needs of pupils with SEN/LDD;

- engage with the *ECM* procedures and protocols such as information sharing, the Common Assessment Framework, the National Service Framework and the team around the child.

The book can be worked through systematically in chapter order, or it can be dipped into, providing a useful point of reference for those wishing to focus on particular topics or aspects of SEN, disability, inclusion and *ECM*. Each chapter provides a summary of what will be covered; key information; practical examples of the national professional and occupational standards related to SEN, disability and *ECM* in action; models of good practice and templates which can be customised and adapted to suit the type of education setting trainee and newly qualified teachers and TAs are working in. Useful resources to signpost the reader to other sources of information, as well as further activities for assignments, reflection and professional development, are provided at the end of every chapter.

The book provides an essential resource that can be used:

- to act as a point of reference for busy trainee and newly qualified teachers and teaching assistants, including induction tutors and newly appointed SENCOs;

- to inform a more consistent, responsive approach to meeting the needs of pupils with SEN/LDD;

- to enable pages to be photocopied for developmental purposes within the purchasing institution or service;

- to promote further discussions and encourage reflection on policy and and practice in relation to SEN, disability, inclusion and *ECM*;

- to support the SEN and *ECM* modules of training and induction programmes for ITT students, NQTs and TAs new to the role.

Introduction

There continues to be a growing commitment to meeting the needs of pupils with special educational needs (SEN) and disabilities in the twenty-first century. The last ten years have seen a plethora of legislation, government and national strategies, and guidance on the well-being and inclusion of children and young people with learning difficulties and/or disabilities (LDD), a term used by Ofsted to refer to SEN pupils in mainstream schools and early years settings. Since this book was first published in 2000, the volume of new legislation and developments in SEN and disability have made this second edition essential.

Removing Barriers to Achievement. The Government's Strategy for SEN (DfES 2004b) acknowledged that trainee and newly qualified teachers would be expected to demonstrate that they:

- understand their responsibilities under the SEN Code of Practice

- differentiate and plan their teaching to meet the needs of pupils, including those with SEN

- identify and support pupils who experience behavioural, emotional and social difficulties

- prevent discrimination against disabled pupils

- spend time with the school's SENCO to focus on specific and general SEN matters (DfES 2004b: 57; paragraph 3.11).

The same government document clarified the role of the teaching assistant or learning support assistant (LSA) working with SEN children: 'It is important that teachers and LSAs play complementary roles . . . whilst making due allowance for special needs, it is important that children do not rely excessively on the LSA or solely on one-to-one help' (DfES 2004b, 60; paragraph 3.16).

Ofsted in its report entitled *Special Educational needs and Disability: Towards Inclusive Schools* found that: 'support by teaching assistants can be vital, but the organisation of it can mean that pupils have insufficient opportunity to develop their skills, under-standing and independence' (Ofsted 2004: 5).

The Professional Standards for Teachers (TDA 2007a) and the National Occupational Standards for Supporting Teaching and Learning in Schools (TDA 2007c) are under-pinned by the *Every Child Matters* five outcomes and they reflect the common core of skills and knowledge for the children's workforce which cover:

- effective communication and engagement with children, young people, parents and carers;
- child and young person development;
- safeguarding and promoting the welfare of the child;
- supporting transitions;
- multi-agency working;
- sharing information.

Both sets of standards for teachers and teaching assistants were revised in 2007 in light of the need to bring them into line with the Workforce Remodelling National Agreement (WRNA) requirements, whereby schools would broaden the roles of their support staff to deliver the core universal offer for extended services.

The Qualified Teacher Status (QTS) Standards, the Induction Standards for Newly Qualified Teachers (NQTs) and the National Occupational Standards (NOS) for Supporting Teaching and Learning, which are relevant to TAs, all have specific requirements related to meeting the needs of pupils with SEN/LDD in schools. These address the recommendation made by the Ofsted HMI report in 2006 entitled *Inclusion: Does It Matter Where Pupils Are Taught? Provision and Outcomes in Different Settings for Pupils with Learning Difficulties and Disabilities*:

> The Training and Development Agency should:
> - improve the initial training and continuing professional development in the field of LDD for all teachers
> - provide more opportunities for specialist training in teaching pupils with learning difficulties in general and for particularly complex disabilities.
>
> (Ofsted 2006a: 4)

The report went on to describe the characteristics of effective, focused professional development for staff in enabling them to meet the needs of pupils with LDD:

> Specific training from specialist teachers and professionals from other agencies was particularly effective, but needed to be regular. . . .
> . . . In-school support, such as coaching, team teaching, mentoring, focused support and management interventions, was particularly effective in building the capacity to provide for pupils with BESD.
>
> (Ofsted 2006a: 10, paragraph 26; 11, paragraph 27)

The government's inclusion development programme (IDP) of web-based materials for trainee and qualified teachers, launched through the National Strategies in 2007, was seen as taking forward the commitment made in *Removing Barriers to Achievement* by providing a four-year programme of continuing professional development (CPD) to increase the confidence and expertise of mainstream practitioners in schools and early years settings in meeting high incidence of SEN.

This book will provide an excellent complementary resource to the government's IDP. It will also include essential information about the *Every Child Matters* (ECM) strategy and how trainee and newly qualified teachers and TAs can meet the requirements of the Change for Children Programme. Overall, this valuable book brings together in one volume all the latest information on SEN, disability, inclusion and *ECM* that is necessary to ensure that trainee and newly qualified teachers and teaching assistants secure better learning and well-being outcomes for the SEN/LDD pupils they work with.

Working within the law and frameworks for SEN, disability and *ECM*

This chapter will cover:

- Professional and occupational standards for teachers and TAs in relation to SEN, disability and *ECM*
- Demystifying the terminology
- Legislation relating to SEN, disability and *ECM* in the twentieth and twenty-first centuries
- Government frameworks and codes of practice for SEN and inclusion
- Government reports and other recent research reports on SEN and inclusion
- Useful resources relating to SEND, inclusion and *ECM* policy and legislation
- Further activities

Professional and occupational standards for teachers and TAs in relation to SEN, disability and *ECM*

According to TDA (2007a), the work of practising teachers, including trainee and newly qualified teachers and TAs, has to be informed by an awareness of:

- the legislation concerning the development and well-being of children and young people expressed in the Children Act 2004;
- the Disability Discrimination Acts 1995 and 2005 and the relevant associated guidance;
- the special educational needs provisions in the Education Act 1996 and the associated Special Educational Needs Code of Practice 2001;
- Guidance on Safeguarding Children in Education (2004).

See Table 1.1.

Demystifying the terminology

Understanding the definition of special educational needs, disability and inclusion is essential for all trainee and newly qualified teachers and TAs. The definitions are clarified in legislation and/or in government guidance. In addition, the glossary at the

Table 1.1

National standards for teachers and TAs on law and frameworks

QTS standards	Induction standards for NQTs	National occupational standards for TAs
Health and well-being Q21 (a) Be aware of the current legal requirements, national policies and guidance on the safeguarding and promotion of the well-being of children and young people. **Learning environment** Q30 Establish a purposeful and safe learning environment conducive to learning and identify opportunities for learners to learn in out-of-school contexts.	**Working within the law and frameworks** C22 Know the current legal requirements, national policies and guidance on the safeguarding and promotion of the well-being of children and young people. C23 Know the local arrangements concerning the safeguarding of children and young people. C24 Know how to identify potential child abuse or neglect and follow safeguarding procedures. C37 (a) Establish a purposeful and safe learning environment which complies with current legal requirements, national policies and guidance on the safeguarding and well-being of children and young people so that learners feel secure and sufficiently confident to make an active contribution to learning and to the school. C37 (b) Make use of the local arrangements concerning the safeguarding of children and young people.	**NVQ Level 2** STL3 Help to keep children safe (keep children safe during day-to-day work activities; deal with accidents, emergencies and illness; support the safeguarding of children from abuse; encourage children's positive behaviour) **NVQ Level 3** STL45 Promote children's well-being and resilience (enable children to take risks safely) STL46 Work with young people to safeguard their welfare (promote a safe working environment; work with young people to assess and manage risk)

Source: TDA (2007a, 2007b, 2007c).

end of this book gives further definitions relating to the different types of learning difficulties and disabilities as defined in the DfES document (2005b) *Data Collection by Type of Special Educational Need*.

Special educational needs (SEN) are learning difficulties and/or disabilities in children that are significantly greater than in the majority of their peers, that prevent or hinder them from making use of education facilities of a kind generally provided for children in schools or early years settings, and that require special educational provision to be made for them.

Special educational provision is that which is additional to or different from the educational provision generally made for children in mainstream schools and early years settings.

Disability is a physical or mental impairment which has a substantial and long–term adverse effect on a child's or young person's ability to carry out normal daily activities. It includes, for example, sensory impairments, mental illness or mental health problems, learning difficulties, dyslexia, diabetes, epilepsy, severe disfigurements, HIV, multiple sclerosis (MS), ADHD, autism and speech and language impairments.

Learning difficulties and/or disabilities (LDD) is the term generally used across the boundaries of education, health and social services in place of SEN.

Dual or multiple exceptionalities (DME) are characteristic of those children and young people who have a special educational need as well as a gift or talent. The SEN or learning difficulty hinders the effective expression of their high ability or exceptional talent. For example, a pupil with a specific learning difficulty may also have a gift for Science which goes unrecognised because the school has focused its attention on addressing the specific learning difficulty first and foremost.

Additional needs are those of children and young people at risk of poor standards in relation to the *Every Child Matters* (*ECM*) five outcomes, who therefore require extra support from education, health or social services for a limited time or on a longer-term basis.

Vulnerable children/young people are those who are at risk of social exclusion, those who are disadvantaged and those whose life chances are likely to be jeopardised unless action is taken to meet their needs better.

Inclusion describes the process of ensuring equality of learning opportunities for all children and young people, irrespective of their diversity. It is about the quality of children's and young people's experience, how they are helped to learn, achieve and participate fully in the life of their education setting and within the community.

Legislation related to SEN, disability and *ECM* in the twentieth and twenty-first centuries

Trainee and newly qualified teachers, TAs and SENCOs new to their role value having an overview of the recent legislation relating to SEN, disability and *ECM*. Table 1.2 provides a useful summary of the key legislation from 1981 to 2009.

Government frameworks and codes of practice for SEND and inclusion

The government's SEN statutory framework comprises:

- *SEN Code of Practice* (DfES 2001c)
- *SEN Toolkit* (DfES 2001d)
- *Removing Barriers to Achievement: The Government's Strategy for SEN* (DfES 2004b).

The government's inclusion framework comprises:

- The National Curriculum Inclusion Statement (DfEE/QCA 1999a)
- DDA and related Code of Practice, SENDA, DED legislation (2002a, 2005)
- *Pedagogy and Personalisation* (DfES 2007c)
- National Strategies 'Waves' of Intervention (DfES 2005a)
- *Inclusion Development Programme* (DCSF 2008f, 2008g).

It is crucial that trainee and newly qualified teachers and teaching assistants know what they are expected to do in relation to SEND and inclusion policy and practice, as well

Table 1.2

SEN, disability and *ECM* legislation

Legislation	Key features of the legislation
Education Act 1981	This Act became effective in the Education Act 1983. It took into account the recommendations of the Warnock Report 1978. The categories of special educational needs (SEN) disappeared; SEN pupils were to be educated in ordinary mainstream schools; LEAs were to maintain a statement of SEN; SEN was defined and parents were partners.
Education Reform Act 1988	Sections 17, 18 and 19 related specifically to SEN and the curriculum: i.e. modification of the curriculum; disapplication from the National Curriculum; the introduction of SATs. Grant maintained status for schools, the local management of schools (LMS), and open competition between schools for pupils were all introduced.
Children Act 1989	This Act dealt with the care, upbringing and welfare of children, particularly 'looked after children' (LAC), or children with SEN. It introduced supervision orders.
Education Act 1993 (Part III)	This updated the Education Act 1981 by introducing the SEN Tribunal, pupil referral units (PRUs), the concept of the Code of Practice for SEN, and the requirement on schools to report annually to parents on SEN policy and provision.
Code of Practice on the Identification and Assessment of Special Educational Needs 1994	This provided a framework for SEN policy, practice and provision. Schools and local education authorities (LEAs) were to have regard to the recommendations made. There were six sections to the Code of Practice which covered: Section 1: integration, early intervention, partnership, continuum of needs and provision; full access to the National Curriculum; mainstream provision where practicable; Section 2: set out definitions and responsibilities and explained the school-based Stages 1 to 3; Section 3: explained the procedures for statutory assessment of SEN; Section 4: explained the statementing process; Section 5: assessments and statementing for children under 5; Section 6: explained the annual review of statements and transitional reviews 14 to 16.
Disability Discrimination Act 1995 (Part IV)	Schools to report on their arrangements for admitting disabled pupils; schools to indicate the steps taken to prevent disabled pupils from being discriminated against; facilities available to assist school access for disabled pupils (accessibility plan). Disabled pupils to have the right to quality education free from discrimination and segregation.
Education Act 1996 (Part IV)	Part IV of the Act referred to SEN, i.e. to pupils with learning difficulties. Outlined the duty to include SEN pupils in mainstream schools. Clarified the staged approach of the SEN Code of Practice. Explained statutory assessment, the statement process and the appeals procedure for the SEN Tribunal. It clarified that LEAs have six weeks in which to decide whether to make a statutory assessment, ten weeks in which to carry out the assessment, and then a further ten weeks in which to decide whether to issue a statement of SEN, and two weeks to inform parents of their decision. Parents to receive a proposed statement and within fifteen days of receiving that statement to decide if it is appropriate and acceptable. If not, parents given a further fifteen days to make their comments. This act was updated in January 1999.
Special Educational Needs and Disability Act 2001	This Act amended the Disability Discrimination Act 1995 by inserting a new Part IV, which prevents discrimination against disabled people in their access to education. From September 2002, it became unlawful to discriminate against disabled pupils and prospective pupils in the provision of education and associated services in schools, and in relation to admissions and exclusions. The Act supports the two Codes of Practice: one for schools, and the other for the post-16 education sector. Section 1 of

Table 1.2 continued

SEN, disability and *ECM* legislation

Legislation	Key features of the legislation
	the Act amends Section 316 of the Education Act 1996 by inserting a new Section 316A relating to 'education otherwise' than in mainstream schools.
Special Educational Needs Code of Practice 2001	This revised SEN Code of Practice became effective in January 2002. It provides a clear framework for identifying, assessing and meeting the needs of pupils with SEN, and it replaced the 1994 version. The new SEN Code of Practice is based on the general principles introduced by the SEN and Disability Act 2001. These principles are: a SEN child should have their needs met, and normally in a mainstream school; the child's views should be considered; parents have a vital role to play in supporting their child's education; and SEN children should have full access to a broad, balanced and relevant curriculum. The Code recommends schools adopt a graduated approach through Early Years Action/School Action and Early Years Action Plus/School Action Plus, and then to a Statement of SEN, where appropriate. The Code's ten chapters cover: principles and policies; working in partnership with parents; pupil participation; identification, assessment and provision in early education settings, in the primary phase and the secondary sector; statutory assessment of SEN; statements of SEN; annual review; and working in partnership with other agencies. The SEN Code of Practice supports SEN pupils in reaching their full potential and making a successful transition to adulthood. The Code is also supported by a separate SEN Toolkit, which provides detailed advice and examples of good practice to schools and LEAs.
The Children Act 2004	This Act was established on 15 November 2004. It brought in important legislation to improve children's and young people's *ECM* well-being outcomes, particularly those of vulnerable children/young people. It covered: the appointment of a national Children's Commissioner to champion the views and interests of children and young people; LAs to make arrangements to promote cooperative joint working between agencies and organisations, through Children's Trusts and local partnership agreements; strengthening the safeguarding and promoting the welfare of children and young people by LAs setting up Local Safeguarding Children Boards; the provision of an index and database for sharing information (e.g. ContactPoint), and the Integrated Children's System; the introduction of the Common Assessment Framework (CAF) for the early assessment of a child/young person's additional needs; the introduction of the National Service Framework for Children, Young People and Maternity Services (NSF); the creation of an integrated inspection framework for LAs; provisions relating to foster care, private fostering and the education of children in care; establishment of Children's Centres and the expansion of the Extended School programme; establishment of a set of core skills and knowledge for the children's workforce; LAs to have a single Children and Young People's Plan, to have a Director of Children's Services and a Lead Member of the council responsible for children and young people.
Disability Discrimination Act 2005	This Act builds on and extends the earlier disability discrimination legislation of 1995. It extended the definition of disability to include those with HIV, multiple sclerosis and some forms of cancer. It also moved away from a mental illness having to be clinically well recognised. This Act gives the disabled rights in the areas of employment, education, access to goods and facilities, services, transport and property. This Act brought in the Disability Equality Duty (the Duty), which includes a general duty and a specific duty, both of which apply to schools, academies and PRUs. The general duty requires schools to have regard to the need to: eliminate unlawful discrimination against the disabled; promote equal opportunities for the disabled; eliminate disability-related harassment; promote positive attitudes towards the disabled; encourage participation by the disabled; and take steps to meet the needs of the disabled, even if

Table 1.2 continued

SEN, disability and *ECM* legislation

Legislation	Key features of the legislation
	this requires more favourable treatment. The general duty applies to disabled pupils, staff and parents/carers and other users of the school. The specific duty requires schools to prepare and publish a disability equality scheme; to involve the disabled in the development of this scheme; implement the Disability Equality Duty Scheme by 3 December 2007; report on it annually, and revise the scheme every three years. Parents can appeal to the independent Special Educational Needs and Disability Tribunal (SENDIST) if a school or other education setting fails to comply with the Disability Equality Duty.
Education and Inspections Act 2006	In relation to SEN and *ECM*, the Act: clarified the role of the SENCO and the requirement for them to be a qualified teacher; ensured fair access to schools irrespective of ability, social background, ethnicity or disability; placed a duty on governing bodies to promote well-being and community cohesion and to take the LA Children and Young People's Plan into consideration; created a power for staff to discipline pupils; extended the scope of parenting orders and contracts; improved the provision for excluded pupils; established new nutritional standards for food and drink being served in maintained schools; merged several inspectorates into a single inspectorate to cover the full range of services for children and young people, as well as lifelong learning. It also expects LAs to promote choice, diversity, high standards and the fulfilment of potential for every child and young person, as well as ensuring young people have a range of exciting and positive things to do in their spare time.
Special Educational Needs (Information) Act 2008	This Act covers information relating to all the five *ECM* well-being outcomes for SEN children and young people. The Act requires the Secretary of State for Education to secure the provision of information about children in England with SEN that would be likely to assist in improving their well-being, and to publish, or arrange to be published, information likely to assist in improving the well-being of children in England with SEN every calendar year. The information to be collected by LAs and schools on the five *ECM* outcomes in relation to learners with SEN/LDD, focus on indicators relating to the revised *ECM* Outcomes Framework, and the progression of SEN learners on transition from EYFS through to the age of 19. This aligns with the Ofsted indicators for measuring a school's contribution to the well-being of their children. The overall aim of collecting *ECM* outcomes information for SEN children and young people (CYP) is that it will help LAs and schools to understand the reasons why CYP with SEN achieve disproportionately poor *ECM* well-being outcomes, and will inform future action for improvement.

as understanding what is feasible to do in the context of the classroom. Providing a more in-depth focus on the requirements of the SEN and the Disability Discrimination Codes of Practice will clarify what NQTs and TAs new to their role need to know, and what these entail and look like in practice.

Special Educational Needs Code of Practice

The duty to observe the SEN Code of Practice continues for its lifetime. The Code sets out guidance on policies and procedures aimed at enabling children and young people with SEN to reach their full potential; to be fully included in their school/ setting's community; and to make a successful transition through to adulthood.

All early years settings, maintained nurseries, mainstream and special schools, academies, technology colleges and PRUs must have a written SEN policy that is kept under regular review, evaluated and revised to reflect any changes in legislation or provision. Trainee and newly qualified teachers and TAs must make themselves familiar with this policy, as it will inform their practice.

The fundamental principles of the SEN Code of Practice are:

- Children with special educational needs should have their needs met.
- The special educational needs of children will normally be met in mainstream schools or early years settings.
- The views of the child should be sought and taken into account.
- Parents have a vital role to play in supporting their child's education.
- Children with SEN should be offered full access to a broad, balanced and relevant education, including an appropriate curriculum for the early years foundation stage and the National Curriculum.

The SEN Code of Practice emphasises that provision for pupils with SEN is the role and responsibility of every teacher. In practice this means that they should:

- identify and reduce the barriers to pupils' learning and participation;
- differentiate the curriculum to provide maximum access;
- follow the guidance of the national primary and secondary strategies and the EYFS on including children and young people with SEN;
- agree individual education plan (IEP) targets with the pupil, parents and the SENCO;
- ensure the SEN pupil knows what their IEP targets are;
- implement the IEP and review it termly, or at least every six months;
- discuss SEN pupil progress with the SENCO and other colleagues working with the same pupil, including external practitioners;
- ensure teacher planning clarifies the deployment and role of additional adults such as TAs and speech and language therapists;
- ensure personalised learning approaches meet SEN pupils' needs;
- monitor the ongoing progress of SEN pupils they teach or support;
- measure SEN pupil progress at the end of a key stage or academic year against National Curriculum or P scale attainment level descriptors;
- work in partnership with SEN pupils' parents/carers, keeping them informed about their child's progress.

Important note

The SEN Code of Practice acknowledges that children and young people with SEN make progress at different rates and have different ways in which they learn best. It must not be assumed that children who are making slower progress or experiencing difficulties in one area necessarily have a special educational need.

The SEN Code of Practice adopts a graduated response to meeting the needs of SEN pupils, which includes: Early Years Action/School Action; Early Years Action Plus/School Action Plus; and, following a successful statutory assessment outcome, a Statement of SEN. These particular responses concern provision and interventions that are **additional to** or **different from** those provided as part of the school's/setting's usual differentiated curriculum offer and differentiated learning opportunities, i.e. above and beyond 'quality-first teaching' (QFT) and personalised learning for all pupils.

Table 1.3 provides a quick guide to the SEN Code of Practice for busy trainee and newly qualified teachers and teaching assistants.

Table 1.3

A quick guide to the SEN Code of Practice

Early Years Action/School Action	Early Years Action Plus/School Action Plus
Triggers for action/intervention The child/young person: • makes little or no progress even when teaching approaches are targeted particularly in their identified area of weakness • continues working at levels significantly below those expected of peers the same age • has difficulty developing literacy or mathematical skills, which result in poor attainment in some areas • presents persistent emotional or behavioural difficulties and fails to respond to behaviour management strategies usually used in the school/setting • has sensory or physical problems, and continues to make little or no progress despite the provision of specialist equipment • has communication and/or interaction difficulties and continues to make little or no progress despite the provision of a differentiated curriculum	**Triggers for action/intervention** The child/young person: • continues to make little or no progress in specific areas over a long period • continues working at National Curriculum levels substantially below those expected of children of a similar age • continues to have difficulty in developing literacy and/or mathematical skills • has emotional or behavioural difficulties which interfere substantially and regularly with their own learning or that of the class group, despite having an individualised behaviour management programme • has sensory or physical needs, and requires additional specialist equipment or regular advice or visits by a specialist service • has ongoing communication or interaction difficulties that impede the development of social relationships and cause substantial barriers to learning
Action to be taken/additional or different provision • The SENCO assesses the child or young person, plans support, and monitors and reviews progress in partnership with the class/subject teacher • The SENCO co-ordinates planning of the child/young person's IEP and sets targets with the class/subject teacher who subsequently implements the IEP • The class/subject teacher remains responsible for working with the child/young person on a daily basis, and for planning and delivering an individualised programme, which is usually delivered by TAs/LSAs or specialist SEN teachers; they also differentiate learning materials, make use of specialist equipment/aids, and deploy TA/LSA to undertake in-class support	**Action to be taken/additional or different provision** • External specialists/practitioners provide further specialist assessment, and/or direct interventions/provision • External specialists will offer advice on IEPs and target setting, teaching approaches and materials, useful resources/ICT • The class/subject teacher implements the IEP • The class/subject teacher is responsible for seeing that the intervention/provision stated on the IEP is delivered • The class/subject teacher, SENCO and other external practitioners involved monitor and evaluate the impact of the additional provision/interventions • If after two IEP reviews there has been significant improvement and the child/young person has made

Table 1.3 continued

A quick guide to the SEN Code of Practice

Early Years Action/School Action	Early Years Action Plus/School Action Plus
• The class/subject teacher identifies and utilises appropriate methods of access to the curriculum being taught • The class/subject teacher and SENCO will collect new additional information about the child/young person, particularly in relation to their progress, and the effectiveness and impact of additional interventions/provision • After two IEP reviews, if the child/young person has made good progress leading to significant improvements which enable them to catch up with their peers, then they will move off the Action stage and off the SEN Register, as they no longer require additional and/or different provision/interventions • If, after two IEP reviews the child/young person has made less than satisfactory/inadequate progress, or progress has deteriorated, the recommendation is made to move them on to Action Plus NB: There may be some instances where a child/young person's special educational needs necessitate them to move directly on to Action Plus, without actually accessing the Action stage.	good progress, then they will revert back to Action stage, with the aim of eventually moving off the Action threshold and off the SEN register • If after two IEP reviews the child/young person's progress is less than satisfactory/inadequate, or has deteriorated, the school/setting and the parents/carers can request the local authority to make a statutory assessment, with a view to obtaining a note in lieu or a statement of SEN

Statutory assessment	Statement of SEN

• Robust evidence has to be provided by the school/setting which proves why the additional interventions and provision at Action and Action Plus have not been successful in addressing the child's/young person's special educational needs. The evidence includes the following:
  – IEPs with their review evidence at Action/Action Plus
  – rates of progress the SEN child/young person has made in relation to their starting points, prior attainment, personal circumstances
  – attainment in literacy and mathematics
  – evidence from other educational assessments
  – evidence of the outcomes from any interventions or additional provision delivered
  – the views of the child/young person about their progress, needs, provision
  – the views of the parents/carers of the child/young person with SEN
  – the views of staff/external practitioners
  – evidence, where appropriate, of the child's/young person's medical history
• The child/young person remains at Action Plus during statutory assessment
	• A statement of SEN is for those children and young people with severe and complex needs who require frequent, regular, daily involvement, support, specialist teaching/equipment, beyond that of a school's or setting's existing provision
	
	• Where it has been agreed to issue a statement of SEN by the LA, the parents/carers receive a draft proposed statement, and they are given time to consider this and make any comments
	
	• From the time the parents/carers receive the initial draft proposed statement it takes eight weeks for the statement of SEN to be finalised by the LA
	
	• The statement of SEN is a legal document that must be acted upon
	
	• The statement of SEN sets out the long-term targets, as well as the short-term targets, in the child/young person's IEP
	
	• The statement of SEN specifies the nature of the child/young person's special educational needs as well as detailing the provision from the school/setting and the LA
	
	• The statement of SEN also states the objectives to be met; the arrangements for monitoring the child/young person's progress; the type and name of the school or education otherwise than at a school; the non-educational needs and non-educational provision such as transport, specialist aids, speech and language therapy
	
	• The statement of SEN must be reviewed annually. The review will include the class/form teacher, SENCO, TA/LSA, learning mentor, the child/young person, their parents/carers, and any external professionals working with the child/young person and their family. The review meeting will consider the progress made by the child/young person and whether the provision should change, remain the same or be discontinued

Table 1.3 continued

A quick guide to the SEN Code of Practice

Statutory assessment	Statement of SEN

• The LA has six weeks in which to consider whether to undertake a statutory assessment
• The LA has ten weeks in which to undertake a statutory assessment
• The LA will request reports and assessments to support the school/setting's evidence from multi-agency services, as appropriate
• Following statutory assessment the LA has two weeks in which to notify the parents/carers of their decision to issue a note in lieu or a statement of SEN
• A note in lieu recommends the appropriate SEN provision for a child/young person not considered to have severe and complex needs
• The entire statutory assessment and statement process takes 26 weeks in total
	• The statement of SEN can be amended, cease to be maintained if:
	  – the objectives of the statement have been met
	  – the child's/young person's special educational needs no longer impede curriculum access
	  – the child's/young person's needs can be met within the setting/school's own resources
	  – daily adult supervision/support or adaptation is no longer required
	  – the child/young person can cope socially and has no significant self-help difficulties

Individual education plans

The individual education plan (IEP) was identified by the SEN Code of Practice as being a teaching and planning tool that outlines three or four individual SEN pupil learning targets, states the appropriate strategies for additional or different provision, and records the outcomes from a review of the provision. It was a method by which schools could comply with the statutory framework and have regard to the SEN Code of Practice.

However, the government in its *SEN Update 18* (DfES 2005e) in November 2005 clarified that IEPs are not a statutory requirement, and that where schools have a robust provision-mapping system comprising individual pupil target setting, planning, tracking, recording and reviewing *all* pupils' progress and outcomes, then SEN pupils should not need an IEP.

Code of Practice for Schools – Disability Discrimination Act 1995 (Part IV)

The Disability Discrimination Act (DDA) 1995 (Part IV), as amended by the Special Educational Needs and Disability Act (SENDA) 2001, Code of Practice for Schools, which became effective from September 2002, set out new duties that local authorities, maintained nursery schools, and maintained and independent schools must follow. These duties, which apply to trainee and newly qualified teachers and teaching assistants, were:

1 not to discriminate against disabled children and prospective pupils in admissions, exclusions, education and associated services which include:

- preparation for entry to school and preparation for moving on to the next phase of education;
- the curriculum, homework, timetabling and activities to supplement the curriculum;

- teaching and learning, classroom organisation, grouping of pupils, assessment and examination arrangements, interaction with peers;
- school policies, access to school facilities, breaks and lunchtimes, the serving of school meals, the school's arrangements for working with other agencies;
- school discipline and sanctions, exclusion procedures;
- school clubs and activities, school sports, school trips;

2 not to treat disabled children less favourably, without justification, for a reason which relates to their disability or impairment;

Example of less favourable treatment but with justification

A pupil with cerebral palsy who is a wheelchair user goes on a school trip with his class to an outdoor education centre. The class are to go on a twelve-mile hike over difficult terrain. The wheelchair user is unable to do the twelve-mile hike for health and safety reasons. Therefore, the class teacher has planned an alternative activity, with additional support from a teaching assistant. Although less favourable treatment may have been shown in this instance, it was justified on the grounds of health and safety, and a reasonable adjustment has been made, to ensure the pupil is included with his peers in an outdoor education experience/learning opportunity.

---

3 to take reasonable steps and make reasonable adjustments to policies, practice and procedures in order to ensure that children and young people with disabilities are not placed at a substantial disadvantage compared to other children/young people who are not disabled. When considering what is 'reasonable' the following factors should be taken into account:

- whether taking the step would be effective in overcoming the incompatibility;
- the extent to which it is practical to take the step;
- the extent to which steps have already been taken to facilitate the child/young person's inclusion, and their effectiveness;
- the financial and other resource implications of taking the step; and
- the extent of any disruption taking the step would cause;

Example of reasonable steps/reasonable adjustments

A 5-year-old child with a medical condition is incontinent and requires nappies to be changed throughout the day at school. The school installs changing facilities in the disabled toilet. It has health and safety procedures in place for dealing with any incontinence issues. A teaching assistant (TA) has been assigned specifically to meet the child's personal needs. The TA has been trained and has received advice and guidance from external professionals about the management of the child's personal needs.

---

4 to plan strategically for, and make progress in, improving the physical environment of schools and maintained early years settings for children with disabilities, increasing their participation in the curriculum and improving the ways in which written information is provided to children, young people and adults with disabilities, in a range of alternative formats, such as in Braille, large print type formats, on audio tape, using signing and symbols to convey information.

The school's accessibility plan outlines what actions it will take to improve access for disabled pupils and adults, in relation to these four aspects.

Inclusive classroom practice and disability access arrangements

In relation to class/subject teachers' classroom practice and TAs' learning support, providing for pupils with disabilities and/or medical needs to have good access to learning and participation, they must ensure that they:

- give additional time, where appropriate, to enable pupils to complete tasks and activities;

- modify/personalise teaching and learning to meet their needs;

- take account of the disabled child's/young person's pace of learning and the specialist aids and equipment they use;

- take account of the effort and concentration needed by the disabled child/young person when undertaking oral work or when using visual aids;

- ensure work is adapted or offer alternative activities in those subjects where children are expected to manipulate tools or equipment, or to use certain types of materials;

- allow opportunities for them to take part in educational visits and out-of-school-hours extra-curricular and extended school activities;

- include approaches that allow those with hearing impairments to learn about sound in Science and Music, and those with visual impairments to learn about light in Science, and to use visual resources and images both in Art and Design and in Design Technology;

- use assessment for learning techniques appropriate to the individual needs and abilities of the child/young person with disabilities and/or medical needs.

Figure 1.1 provides a useful checklist for trainee and newly qualified teachers and teaching assistants to use as a point of reference, in order to ensure that disabled children and young people have physical access and curriculum access as well as access to information in alternative formats.

The National Curriculum inclusion statement of principles

The National Curriculum statutory inclusion statement was first published in 1999, with the programmes of study and attainment targets from Key Stage 1 through to Key Stage 4 (DfEE QCA 1999a, 1999b). The QCA provides a useful chart to support this statutory inclusion statement, which demonstrates how different groups of pupils, including those with SEN and disability, can be included in the curriculum. The chart, entitled 'Including All Learners', can be downloaded at http://www.qca.org.uk/ library/Assets/media/including_all_learners_A3.pdf

Curriculum access	YES	NO
The training you have had has helped you to teach and support disabled children	☐	☐
Your classroom/support area is well organised to accommodate disabled children	☐	☐
Your lessons/interventions provide opportunities for disabled children to achieve along with other children	☐	☐
Your lessons/interventions are responsive to children's/young people's diversity	☐	☐
Your lessons/interventions feature individual, pair, group and whole class work	☐	☐
All children, including the disabled, are encouraged to take part in drama, music, PE	☐	☐
You recognise and allow for the mental effort expended by some disabled children in undertaking tasks and activities	☐	☐
You recognise and allow for the additional time required by some disabled children to use equipment in practical work	☐	☐
You provide alternative ways of giving access to experiences or understanding for disabled children who cannot engage in particular activities	☐	☐
You provide sufficient access to ICT and other forms of technology for children with disabilities	☐	☐
You make educational visits, residential experiences and school holidays accessible to children with disabilities	☐	☐
You have high expectations of children with disabilities and/or medical needs	☐	☐

Classroom/learning support environment access	YES	NO
Children with disabilities sit near the front of the class/group	☐	☐
Access around the classroom/learning support area is good for disabled children and/or wheelchair users	☐	☐
The classroom/learning support area provides clear signing/notices about safety in alternative formats for disabled children, e.g. symbols, tactile buttons	☐	☐
All areas of the classroom/learning support area are appropriately illuminated	☐	☐
The classroom/learning support area has appropriate acoustics to reduce background noise for those children with hearing impairments	☐	☐
Classroom/learning support area furniture and equipment are adjusted in height and located appropriately for children with disabilities and/or wheelchair users	☐	☐

Information/materials accessibility	YES	NO
You provide information in simple language and in alternative formats, e.g. use symbols, large print, Braille, audio tape, for those children/adults who may have difficulty with standard forms of printed information	☐	☐
You ensure that information is presented to groups in a way that is user-friendly for those with disabilities, e.g. by reading aloud information from an interactive whiteboard computer screen/website, and describing diagrams	☐	☐
You have access to ICT facilities to enable you to produce written information in different formats	☐	☐
You ensure that any other teaching or learning support staff working with you are familiar with technology and practices developed to assist children with disabilities	☐	☐

Figure 1.1 Checklist for identifying barriers to access for disabled children

From Rita Cheminais (2010), *Special Educational Needs for Newly Qualified Teachers and Teaching Assistants*, 2nd edn. London: Routledge. © 2010 Rita Cheminais

The National Curriculum statutory inclusion statement sets out three principles for developing an inclusive curriculum which schools must follow. These are:

- to set suitable learning challenges;

- to respond to pupils' diverse learning needs;

- to overcome potential barriers to learning and assessment for individuals and groups of pupils.

Figure 1.2 illustrates the three National Curriculum inclusion principles in practice. An inclusive curriculum is one where:

- different groups of pupils are all able to see the relevance of the curriculum to their own experiences and aspirations;

- all pupils, regardless of ability, have sufficient opportunities to succeed in their learning at the highest standard.

Inclusion is concerned with:

- the quality of a pupil's experience;

- providing access to a high-quality education which enables pupils to make progress in their learning;

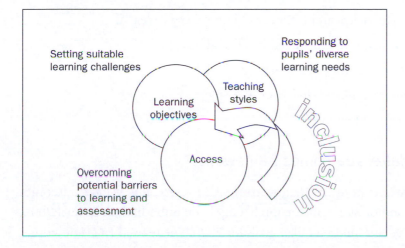

Setting suitable learning challenges	Responding to pupils' diverse learning needs	Overcoming potential barriers to learning and assessment
Teachers/TAs should: · give every learner the opportunity to experience success in learning and achieving as high a standard as possible · teach the knowledge, skills and understanding in ways that match and suit pupils' different abilities · adopt a flexible approach to take account of any gaps in pupils' learning.	Teachers/TAs should: · create effective learning environments · secure pupils' motivation and concentration · provide equality of opportunity through teaching approaches · use appropriate assessment approaches · set appropriate targets for learning.	Teachers/TAs should: · support pupils to enable them to participate effectively in curriculum and assessment activities · plan the curriculum and assessment for pupils with SEND by taking account of the type and extent of the difficulty and disability experienced by the pupil.

Figure 1.2 National Curriculum statutory inclusion statement of principles

- how pupils are helped to learn, achieve and participate fully in the activities and life of their school and community.

The government, in *Removing Barriers to Achievement*, acknowledged that: 'Effective inclusion relies on more than specialist skills and resources. It requires positive attitudes towards children who have difficulties in schools, a greater responsiveness to individual needs and critically, a willingness among all staff to play their part' (DfES 2004b: 32; paragraph 2.7).

Inclusion is an ongoing process focused on the presence, participation and achievement of the full diversity of learners within the classroom/educational setting. The concept of inclusion is based on a set of guiding principles, whereby all children and young people, regardless of their ability, gender, language or ethnic or cultural origin, are valued equally, treated with respect and provided with real opportunities in the early years setting/school.

Inclusion takes a holistic approach to meeting the individual needs of learners. It relies on the following essential characteristics:

- flexible curriculum provision;
- personalised learning and personalised services tailored to meet learners' diverse needs;
- effective deployment of additional adult support;
- flexible teaching approaches and teaching children how to learn;
- commitment to inclusion that is shared by all staff;
- careful assessment of assessment for learning;
- focus on outcomes for children and young people;
- an ethos of acceptance of all pupils.

The *Every Child Matters* outcomes framework

There have been three versions of the government's *Every Child Matters* outcomes framework, the third and most recent version having been published on 3 April 2008, to reflect the government's Children's Plan goals for 2020. The revised *ECM* outcomes framework is available at http://www.everychildmatters.gov.uk/aims/outcomes/

The *ECM* outcomes framework is based on five well-being outcomes for all children and young people, which were identified in the *Every Child Matters* Green Paper (DfES 2003a). Children and young people with SEN and disabilities constitute one of the government's target groups for improving *ECM* outcomes. The *ECM* outcomes framework supports the government's SEN strategy. Table 1.4 provides a comprehensive overview of the five *ECM* outcomes.

Safeguarding children in education

The government's *Every Child Matters* strategy and the Children Acts of 1989 and 2004 defined safeguarding and promoting the welfare of children as entailing:

- protecting children from maltreatment;
- preventing impairment of children's health and development;

Table 1.4

Summary of the *Every Child Matters* outcomes framework

ECM outcomes	Be healthy	Stay safe	Enjoy and achieve	Make a positive contribution	Achieve economic well-being
ECM aims	• Physically healthy • Mentally and emotionally healthy • Sexually healthy • Healthy lifestyles • Choose not to take illegal drugs	• Safe from maltreatment, neglect, violence and sexual exploitation • Safe from accidental injury and death • Safe from bullying and discrimination • Safe from crime and anti-social behaviour in and out of school • Have security, stability and care	• Ready for school • Attend and enjoy school • Achieve stretching national educational standards at primary school • Achieve personal and social development and enjoy recreation • Achieve stretching national educational standards at secondary school	• Engage in decision making and support the community and environment • Engage in law-abiding and positive behaviour in and out of school • Develop positive relationships and choose not to bully and discriminate • Develop self-confidence and deal successfully with significant life changes and challenges • Develop enterprising behaviour	• Engage in further education, employment or training on leaving school • Be ready for employment • Live in decent homes and sustainable communities • Have access to transport and material goods • Live in households free from low income

- ensuring that children grow up in circumstances consistent with the provision of safe and effective care;
- enabling children in need, particularly the vulnerable and disabled, to have optimum life chances, and to enter adulthood successfully.

Revised guidance issued in 2004 saw safeguarding children and young people and promoting their welfare as the duty of all those who come into contact with them in their everyday work in schools. This means that all adults in a school have a role to play in relation to:

- preventing children and young people from being abused;
- promoting the welfare of children and young people;
- preventing children and young people from being harmed;
- acting in the appropriate way if a child/young person makes a disclosure.

Two key aspects of safeguarding and promoting the welfare of children and young people were identified in the guidance. These were:

1 arrangements to take all reasonable measures to ensure that risks of harm to children's welfare are minimised; and

2 arrangements to take all appropriate actions to address concerns about the welfare of a child, or children, working to agreed local policies and procedures in full partnership with other agencies.

Children and young people have the right:

- not to be touched inappropriately;
- not to be physically punished or abused;
- not to be verbally abused;
- to be treated with respect and dignity and with due regard to their privacy;
- to be listened to if they report that they believe an adult has behaved inappropriately.

The role of the school, in instances where there are child protection concerns, is to recognise and refer on to the appropriate agencies, rather than to investigate. Every school is required to nominate a designated teacher for child protection and safeguarding. They, along with the headteacher, are the person to whom trainee or newly qualified teachers and TAs should refer any concerns or disclosures, on the same day as they were made or observed. If neither member of staff is available on that day then another member of the senior leadership team must be informed. Teaching and learning support staff are well placed to observe outward signs of abuse, changes in behaviour, or failure to develop in the children and young people they work with.

Child abuse is usually categorised into four types: physical, sexual, emotional and neglect. Table 1.5 provides an overview of each type.

What to do if a child/young person wants to make a disclosure

The following step-by-step guide will help trainee and newly qualified teachers and teaching assistants to know how to cope with any disclosures and concerns relating to potential or suspected child abuse.

1 Reassure the child/young person that they are right to tell and that they are not to blame for what has happened to them.

2 Do not promise not to tell anyone else but explain to the child/young person that you have to make certain that they are safe, and therefore may need to ask other adults to help you to ensure this happens.

3 Listen to them carefully and do not question the child/young person. Allow them to tell you what they want to tell you and no more.

4 When the child/young person has finished making the disclosure, make sure they feel safe, and explain what you are going to do next.

5 Write down notes on what the child has told you. The notes should include the following information: the date, the time and the place where the disclosure was made. They should also include the names of all adults present when the child/young person made the disclosure. The record of the child/young person's account should

Table 1.5

Types, characteristics and signs of child abuse

Type of abuse	Characteristics of the abuse	Signs of the abuse to look out for
Physical abuse	Hitting, shaking, throwing, poisoning, burning, scalding, drowning, suffocating the child/young person to deliberately cause physical harm to them.	Look out for: unexplained recurrent injuries or burns; improbable excuses or refusal to explain injuries; refusal to undress for PE or sports; aggression towards other peers; chronic running away from school; self-destructive tendencies; fear of physical contact from others – shrinking back if touched; bald patches in their hair.
Sexual abuse	Forcing or enticing a child/young person to take part in sexual activities, including prostitution. It includes physical contact and sexual activities as well as non-contact activities such as forcing the child/young person to look at sexual online images or watch sexual activities in the home. The child/young person, as a result of this abuse, may behave in sexually inappropriate ways.	Look out for: a child/young person being overly affectionate or knowledgeable in a sexual way inappropriate to their age; depression, self-harm, suicide attempts, running away, drug overdoses, compulsive eating or anorexia; personality changes, i.e. insecure or clinging; regressing to younger behaviour, e.g. thumb sucking, cuddling a soft toy; withdrawn, inability to concentrate; overreacting to criticism or trying to be very good/perfect; drawing sexually explicit pictures.
Emotional abuse	Persistent emotional maltreatment of a child/young person which causes severe and persistent adverse effects to their emotional development. It may involve the abuser conveying to the child/young person that they are worthless, unloved, inadequate, unwanted; preventing the child from participating in normal social interaction with their peers. It may involve them seeing or hearing the ill-treatment of another person/child in the family. It may also involve serious bullying, exploitation or corruption of the child/young person.	Look out for: sudden speech disorders; continual putting themselves down, i.e. 'I am stupid, ugly, a waste of space'. Overreaction to making mistakes; extreme fear of any new situation; extremes in behaviour – passive or aggressive; neurotic behaviour such as rocking, hair twisting or self-harm.
Neglect	Failure to meet a child/young person's basic physical, emotional or psychological needs which is likely to result in the serious impairment of their health or development, e.g. where a parent is failing to provide adequate food, clothing, or shelter; or to protect a child from physical and emotional harm or danger; not ensuring adequate supervision of the child at home; not ensuring access to appropriate medical care or treatment.	Look out for: constant hunger; poor personal hygiene; constant tiredness; poor state of clothing; emaciation; untreated medical problems; lack of social relationships with their peers; destructive tendencies.

use their exact words. You must sign the notes and then pass them on immediately to the child protection/safeguarding co-ordinator in school. See Figure 1.3.

6 Ensure that you receive feedback on the outcomes of your referral from the child protection/safeguarding co-ordinator in the school.

Name of child: _____

Date of disclosure: _____

Location of the disclosure: _____

Names of adults present during the disclosure: _____

_____

Exact written account of the disclosure in the child's own words

Signature of adult(s) present: _____

_____

PRINT NAME(S): _____

_____

Role of adult(s) present: _____

_____

Figure 1.3 Template for recording a disclosure

From Rita Cheminais (2010), *Special Educational Needs for Newly Qualified Teachers and Teaching Assistants*, 2nd edn. London: Routledge. © 2010 Rita Cheminais

Trainee and newly qualified teachers and teaching assistants need to be aware that some factors may prevent a child/young person from making a disclosure. These include the following:

- direct threats being made if the child/young person talks to others;
- fear of punishment;
- thinking no one will listen to what they say or take them seriously;
- lack of trust in others;
- fear of the implications of telling, e.g. the family breaking up;
- not realising a situation is abusive or neglectful.

Children and young people are more likely to feel able to make a disclosure when:

- their self-esteem is high;
- their views and contributions are respected;
- there is space for privacy in school;
- the school feels a safe place to be in;
- there is a culture of openness, honesty and trust;
- adults and children/young people in school are respectful to each other;
- staff in school allow children and young people to be heard without interruption.

Government reports and other recent research reports on SEN and inclusion

There have been a large number of reports on SEN and inclusion, particularly in the last ten years. The majority of the reports seek to clarify the definitions of SEN and inclusion, as well as reviewing and reflecting upon whether the government's SEN framework and inclusion policy are actually working.

Table 1.6 provides an overview of the key features of official reports and guidance, while Table 1.7 gives a summary of the main findings from recent research reports. The recent research report findings indicate that the government should review its current SEN framework and its inclusion policy. A summary of the main findings from these research reports indicate that:

- The trend towards LAs issuing fewer statements of SEN is leading to more children and young people who would previously have been given a statement being retained at Action Plus on limited resources.

- Statistics indicate that children and young people with SEN, including those at Action Plus, are more likely to truant, be persistent absentees, or be expelled, suspended or permanently excluded from schools.

- The reduction in special school places has led to more pupils with SEN statements being educated in independent special schools, or being sent to pupil referral units (PRUs). Ofsted in 2006 found PRUs to be the least effective place for children with SEN to be educated. PRUs are intended for short-term use with the aim of pupils eventually being able to return to mainstream schools.

- The Primary Review research (Daniels and Porter 2007) found that differences existed across LAs in relation to the identification and interpretations of SEN.

Table 1.6

Key reports and government guidance on SEN, disability, inclusion and *Every Child Matters* (*ECM*)

Report/guidance title	Key features of the report/guidance
The Report of the Committee of Inquiry into the Education of Handicapped Children and Young People (Warnock 1978)	Also known as the Warnock Report. This report recommended the end of SEN categorisation; promoted the right of all children to be educated, and parents of children with SEN to be partners in their child's education. It brought in the term special educational needs (SEN) to replace the former statutory categories of handicap. The report identified that as many as one in five children (20%) could experience special educational needs at some point in their school career. Warnock in this report introduced the notion of a continuum of need, ranging from temporary difficulties to those which are severe and enduring. The report recommended a system of recording (statementing). The Warnock Report established the term integration identifying three types: locational = provision made on the same site as mainstream peers; social = sharing of social spaces such as a playground and extra-curricular activities; and functional = where children with SEN and mainstream children are educated together, pursuing the same curriculum goals and activities. The report was important because it emphasised that SEN was of importance for all teachers and educationalists, and not just for those in special schools.
Excellence for All Children. Meeting Special Educational Needs (DfEE 1997)	This DfEE Green Paper on SEN covered six main themes: (i) higher expectations for SEN pupils; (ii) supporting parent partnership and strengthening parents of SEN pupils' rights; (iii) increased inclusion opportunities in mainstream schools; (iv) focus on shifting from procedures to practical support for SEN; (v) training and professional development in SEN for teachers, trainee teachers and NQTs – with more multi-agency partnership between health, education and social services encouraged; (vi) promoting partnership in SEN locally, regionally and nationally.
Meeting Special Educational Needs. A Programme of Action (DfEE 1998)	This built on the DfEE Green Paper of 1997. The aim was to improve standards and achievement in SEN. Five themes were featured: (i) working with parents – early identification, early years; (ii) improving the SEN framework – revised SEN Code of Practice, improving IEPs and introducing national standards for SENCOs; (iii) developing a more inclusive education system; (iv) developing knowledge and skills of SEN among teachers, LSAs, educational psychologists (EPs) and school governors; (v) working in partnership to meet SEN – regional co-ordination of SEN provision, improved multi-agency working, and reviewing the work of therapy services, improving post-16 provision for SEN students.
Supporting the Target Setting Process. Guidance for Effective Target Setting for Pupils with Special Educational Needs (DfEE/QCA 1998)	This document details the differentiated performance criteria devised by the DfEE and the QCA for SEN pupils operating below National Curriculum Level 1 (known as P scale levels), and within National Curriculum Levels 1 and 2 (smaller steps 1C, 1B, 1A, 2C, 2B, 2A). The criteria covered language and literacy, mathematics and personal and social development. They provided a common assessment framework which could be used at the end of an academic year or key stage. They also enabled SEN pupils' achievements to be recognised, and offered an alternative to W (working towards) and (D) disapplication.
Social Inclusion (Circular 10/99 and Circular 11/99) (DfEE 1999a, 1999b)	These two circulars focused on improving attendance and behaviour, reducing exclusions/disaffection and providing greater curriculum flexibility, as well as describing pastoral support programmes.
From Exclusion to Inclusion. A Report of the Disability Rights Task Force 1999	Chapter 4 of this report related to education emphasised strengthening mainstream inclusion for disabled children and young people. The report recommended strengthening the rights of parents of children with SEN. It also wanted LEA and school policies, practice and procedures to be adjusted to avoid discrimination on the grounds of disability. In addition, it wanted accessibility to schools and the curriculum to be increased.

Table 1.6 continued

Key reports and government guidance on SEN, disability, inclusion and *Every Child Matters* (*ECM*)

Report/guidance title	Key features of the report/guidance
Evaluating Educational Inclusion (Ofsted 2000)	This Ofsted publication defined an educationally inclusive school as one in which the teaching and learning, achievements, attitudes and well-being of every young person matter; and where their ethos and willingness offer new opportunities to pupils who may have already experienced previous difficulties, i.e. pupils with SEN.
Supporting the Target Setting Process. Guidance for Effective Target Setting for Pupils with SEN (DfEE 2001)	This revised guidance included a further breakdown of levels P1 to P3 into smaller steps: P1(i), P1(ii), P2(i), P2(ii), P3(i), P3(ii). This revised edition omitted Personal and Social Development (PSD) and replaced it with Science. The guidance required special schools and mainstream schools with and without special units to set measurable performance targets for SEN pupils at Key Stages 2, 3 and 4 based on the P scales or other performance criteria as appropriate.
Planning, Teaching and Assessing the Curriculum for Pupils with Learning Difficulties (QCA 2001)	This QCA guidance related to all pupils aged 5 to 16 who were unlikely to achieve above National Curriculum Level 2 when they reached the end of Key Stage 4. There were fifteen booklets in total, two of which covered general guidelines and developing skills. The other thirteen booklets covered all the National Curriculum subjects, plus PSHE and Citizenship, and RE. The guidelines were designed to help schools to develop an inclusive curriculum which responded to pupils' diverse learning needs and overcame potential barriers to learning and assessment. Each subject booklet contained guidance on planning, developing and implementing the curriculum for pupils with learning difficulties. They also contained the performance descriptions (P levels), showing pupils' progress up to National Curriculum Level 1. The guidance and subject booklets were designed to help teachers to recognise attainment and structure to their teaching. The guidelines drew on effective best practice across a range of schools and could be used in mainstream and special schools, and specialised units.
Supporting School Improvement: Emotional and Behavioural Development (QCA 2001a)	This QCA booklet offered guidance on setting improvement targets for pupils' emotional and behavioural development to support school improvement. Part 1 outlined the criteria for assessing pupils' emotional and behavioural development. It also provided guidance on how to use the emotional and behavioural criteria. There are fifteen criteria descriptors in total, five for each of the three aspects: learning behaviour, conduct behaviour and emotional behaviour. Each descriptor has a six-point scale of 0 to 5, with 0 = not at all; 1 = rarely; 2 = sometimes; 3 = fairly often; 4 = often; and 5 = always. Part 2 of the guidance explained the background to the school improvement cycle and how the cycle relates to schools setting additional targets for emotional and behavioural development.
Inclusive Schooling: Children with Special Educational Needs 2001	This statutory guidance provided practical advice on the operation of the new framework for inclusion. All maintained schools, including nursery schools and LEAs, must have regard to the guidance. It provided examples of the steps schools and LEAs should take to ensure that a child or young person's inclusion is not incompatible with the efficient education of other children. The guidance also gave instances when it may not always be possible to include specific children and young people in mainstream schools. The document outlined the safeguards that protect individual SEN children's and all pupils' interests. It defined a dual placement special school pupil (51% or more time in mainstream).
SEN Toolkit (DfES 2001d)	This DfES toolkit was designed to help everyone working with SEN pupils. It needs to be read in conjunction with the SEN Code of Practice. The toolkit provides practical suggestions on ways in which early education settings, schools, LEAs, health and social services could implement the statutory guidance set out in the SEN Code of Practice. The toolkit has twelve sections (booklets) which cover: principles and

Table 1.6 continued

Key reports and government guidance on SEN, disability, inclusion and *Every Child Matters* (*ECM*)

Report/guidance title	Key features of the report/guidance
	policies; parent partnership services; resolution of disagreements; enabling pupil participation; managing IEPs; strands of action to meet SEN; writing a statement of SEN; guidelines for writing advice; preparing for and conducting annual reviews; transition planning; the role of social services; and the role of health professionals. Each section (booklet) includes some key general principles from the SEN Code of Practice.
Special Educational Needs: A Mainstream Issue (Audit Commission 2002)	This report by the Audit Commission was published in November 2002. It looked at how well the education system was serving children with SEN. The report focused on SEN children's experiences in four stages: identifying needs; their presence in relation to being able to attend a mainstream school or early years setting; their participation in respect of SEN children being able to participate fully in the life of their school/early years setting; and their achievement in relation to SEN children enabled to reach their full potential. The report also considered the significant role special schools would continue to play within SEN provision. Overall the key recommendations of the report were: to promote consistent practice in identifying and meeting SEN children's needs; to promote early intervention; to ensure that SEN children are able to attend a local mainstream school as far as possible; to promote effective inter-agency planning and provision; to develop the skills and confidence of staff to respond to the wide range of SEN children's needs in the classroom; to promote the effective allocation and management of SEN resources; to hold schools or their work on SEN to account; to recognise schools' commitment to helping children with SEN to achieve. This report informed the government's response in its publication *Removing Barriers to Achievement: The Government's Strategy for SEN* (2004).
The Report of the Special Schools Working Group (DfES 2003c)	This report highlighted the recommendations from the Special Schools Working Group on how special schools might develop their role further within the wider context of inclusion. It acknowledged that special schools had a leading role to play in helping mainstream schools develop more inclusive learning environments. It outlined the key principles that underpin future inclusion developments in partnerships between special and mainstream schools. These were: to innovate in curricular development to facilitate SEN pupils' inclusion into mainstream schools; to raise expectations in relation to the achievement and attainment of SEN pupils; to provide resource bases for teaching methods, resources and ideas for both special and mainstream schools to utilise; for special schools to be outward-looking centres of excellence and expertise in SEN; to help break down barriers between pupils educated in mainstream and special schools and FE colleges; to encourage staff and pupil movement between special and mainstream schools; to promote collaborative working between special and mainstream schools through federations, clusters and outreach working.
Every Child Matters (DfES 2003a)	This Green Paper published in September 2003 outlined the government's vision and proposals for improving services for all children and young people. It also specified the five *Every Child Matters* (*ECM*) well-being outcomes for children and young people. It proposed a lead professional to be responsible for co-ordinating services to meet a child's additional needs; it introduced the concept of a common assessment framework (CAF) to be used across services; it described the changes it wished to see in local authorities such as a Director of Children's Services instead of an Education Director, and a Lead Member of the elected council for Children's Services; Children's Trusts and Local Safeguarding Children's Boards were to be established. The Green Paper outlined the developments it wished to see made

Table 1.6 continued

Key reports and government guidance on SEN, disability, inclusion and *Every Child Matters* (*ECM*)

Report/guidance title	Key features of the report/guidance
	under Workforce Reform, along with improving the skills, training and effectiveness of the Children's Workforce.
Removing Barriers to Achievement: The Government's Strategy for SEN (DfES 2004b)	The government published this document in February 2004, in response to the Audit Commission's findings in 2002. It sets out to make improvements in SEN policy, practice and provision. The introduction to the SEN strategy identifies four continuing challenges in the Audit Commission's 2002 report: too many children are waiting too long to have their needs met; some SEN children are being turned away from mainstream settings because too many staff feel ill-equipped to meet the wide range of pupil needs in the classroom; many special schools feel unsure about their future role; and families of SEN children face unacceptable variations in the level of support available from their local school, LA or local health service. There were four parts to the document: *Early intervention* – to ensure that children who have learning difficulties receive the help they need as soon as possible and that parents of children with SEND have access to suitable childcare; *Removing barriers to learning* – embedding inclusive practice in every school and early years setting; *Raising expectations and achievement* – developing teachers' skills and strategies for meeting the needs of SEN children and sharpening the focus on the progress made by children with SEN; and *Delivering improvements in partnership* – taking a hands-on approach to improvement so that parents can be confident that their child with SEN will get the education they need. The SEN strategy identified thirty actions for the government to take and implement over 2004 and 2005, in order to improve SEN provision. The government concluded its vision document by stating that a difference will have been made when: SEN children have their needs met early; they feel valued members of the school community; special and mainstream schools work in partnership; and there is greater consistency in the quality of SEN provision.
Every Child Matters: Next Steps (DfES 2004g)	This document, which was published in March 2004, described the government's next steps, following consultation on the Green Paper 2003, towards developing a programme of change for children, and strengthening partnership working across services. It outlined the legislative steps for developing more accountable and accessible services, focused on the needs of children, young people and their families. It brought in the National Service Framework (NSF) for Children, Young People and Maternity Services which introduced a set of evidence-based standards for health, social care and some education services. It also introduced the concept of personalisation in learning, care and support. Finally, this document set out a timetable for the implementation of the legislation in the Children Bill, which subsequently became the Children Act 2004, in November 2004.
Special Educational Needs and Disability. Towards Inclusive Schools (Ofsted 2004)	This Ofsted HMI report was published in October 2004. Its purpose was to examine the extent to which the inclusion framework had had an impact on the capacity of mainstream schools to effectively meet the needs of pupils with a wider range of special educational needs. The report's main findings were: there was a growing awareness of the benefits of inclusion; there had not been an increase in mainstream schools in the range of special educational needs being met; expectations of achievement for SEN pupils were not high or clear enough; few schools evaluated their SEN provision systematically; there were limited data available or used on outcomes for SEN pupils; not enough adaptation of the curriculum or teaching methods was taking place; the organisation of support by TAs did not always help to develop SEN pupils' independence, skills or understanding; over half the schools visited had no disability access plans and those that did exist focused only on accommodation access; the admission of pupils with BESD

Table 1.6 continued

Key reports and government guidance on SEN, disability, inclusion and *Every Child Matters* (*ECM*)

Report/guidance title	Key features of the report/guidance
	continued to challenge the inclusion framework; the attitudes of staff to inclusion in mainstream schools have been slow to shift. Ofsted identified the following factors as enabling mainstream schools to meet special needs very well: high expectations, effective whole-school planning, skilled teachers and support staff paying close attention to the needs of SEN pupils, and rigorous evaluation of SEN provision. Ofsted's overall conclusion was that the inclusion framework had had little impact on the proportion or range of SEN pupils attending mainstream schools. The report in Annex B provided a set of valuable criteria for evaluating SEN provision which related to: SEN pupil progress, curriculum access, teaching and learning, SEN pupil participation, inclusion policy and practice.
Every Child Matters: Change for Children (DfES 2004d)	In December 2004, *Every Child Matters: Change for Children* was published as four complementary documents related specifically to expected changes in schools, social care, the criminal justice system, and health services. *Change for Children* confirmed the national framework for local change programmes necessary for building better services around the needs of children and young people. It also emphasised the importance of listening to the views of children, young people and their families to inform more coherent service planning and improved service delivery. The *Every Child Matters* Outcomes Framework was published (Version 2 in September 2005, and Version 3 in April 2008), which was central to informing the 150 local authorities' change programmes.
Using the P Scales (QCA 2005)	QCA published this DVD pack with an accompanying guidance booklet in July 2005 in response to the revision of the P scales in July 2004. It provided exemplification of the P scale level descriptors in English, Mathematics and Science on DVD, to support the moderation of teacher assessment within and between schools. The guidance is designed for staff in mainstream and special schools to make best fit judgements about pupils' attainments below Level 1 of the National Curriculum. The pack was also designed to help staff in schools have a common understanding of the P scales (differentiated performance criteria) which were to be used for pupils aged 5 to 16. The levels in the P scales operate independently of chronological age: for example, a 7-year-old may attain level P8, while some 16-year-olds with more complex needs may be working at levels P1 to P3. The guidance clarified that P scales were to be used for the following purposes: to support summative assessment of the National Curriculum at the end of a year or key stage; to track individual pupils' linear progress in subjects; to identify and record individual pupils' lateral progress across subjects; to look for patterns in the attainments of pupils and to provide information to support target setting.
Removing Barriers: A 'Can-do' Attitude (Ofsted 2005)	This Ofsted HMI report was published in September 2005. The report looked at developing good practice for children with special needs in early years childcare and education in the private and voluntary sectors. The key findings were: private and voluntary sector providers needed more direction about how to include children with special needs; barriers to inclusion could be overcome if providers had a positive, welcoming and 'can-do' approach to inclusion; children with SEN were more likely to achieve the best outcomes when providers: welcome and work in partnership with their families; understand their own strengths and weaknesses and make plans to extend their provision for children with SEN; use training to raise the awareness, skills and confidence of staff; have access to co-ordinated multi-agency services from health and social services that support children with SEN and their transition to school. They also identified that modest, imaginative and low-cost adaptations to equipment and buildings could also help to remove barriers to inclusion.

Table 1.6 continued

Key reports and government guidance on SEN, disability, inclusion and *Every Child Matters* (*ECM*)

Report/guidance title	Key features of the report/guidance
Special Educational Needs: A New Look (Warnock 2005)	This policy document by Baroness Mary Warnock called for a radical review of special needs education, and reconsideration of the SEN framework. According to Baroness Warnock, statements of SEN needed to be reconsidered and reviewed, as inequalities existed in the provision available across LAs, there was a lack of clarity in the criteria for determining which children get a statement, and the statementing system was over-bureaucratic. Warnock also felt that the government should rethink its inclusion framework because the meaning of inclusion was unclear. She considered that the concept of inclusion was more about 'hearts in the right place', and children being involved in a common enterprise of learning, rather than necessarily being under the same roof. Baroness Warnock called for the government to consider creating smaller specialist schools which could cater for children with specific disabilities, those unable to function in larger schools, and those with needs that arise from social disadvantage, i.e. children in public care (LAC). She called for a government-funded independent Committee of Inquiry into the current state of special education.
House of Commons Education and Skills Committee's Report on Special Educational Needs (TSO 2006a)	This report was published in July 2006. It identified the inherent problems associated with the category and sub-categories of SEN, which were covering a wide range of learning difficulties on a continuum of need. It also stated that there appeared to be considerable confusion existing over the government's position on inclusion and the future of special schools. It observed that it may be timely for the government to review the statementing process. They would like to see absolute deadlines for the decision-making process and making statements transferable between LAs. The Committee had some concerns about the assessment of SEN being made directly by the bodies that fund the provision, i.e. the local authorities. It wanted to see the government giving stronger guidance to LAs on when a statement of SEN should be issued. It agreed with the government that it is better to seek to reduce the reliance on statements of SEN by improving the skills and capacity of mainstream schools to meet a diverse range of needs. In relation to placements and choice the Committee wanted to see a national framework of guidance in place which would help to make local authority SEN provision more uniform. In addition, it wanted to see a broad range of high-quality, well-resourced, flexible provisions to meet the needs of all children with SEN. The report encourages dual placements and the sharing of facilities, specialist resources and expertise between mainstream and special schools. The Committee wanted to see, in the new Code of Practice on School Admissions, children with SEN and disabilities being given explicit priority in over-subscription criteria, as well as academies being put on the same legal footing as all other schools with regard to children with SEN. In relation to initial teacher training (ITT) and continuing professional development (CPD), the Committee suggested good-quality, appropriate CPD should be made available for all teachers, and schools should be resourced to fund them. It wanted to see compulsory in-service training including SEN. The Committee did not see the optional modules on SEN in initial teacher training having a great impact, especially where a large part of ITT one-year courses are largely spent in school. The Committee stated that the SENCO should in all cases be a qualified teacher in a senior management position in the school. They should be able to have ongoing training opportunities to keep their knowledge up to date, as well as having sufficient non-teaching time to reflect the number of children with SEN within their school.

Table 1.6 continued

Key reports and government guidance on SEN, disability, inclusion and *Every Child Matters* (*ECM*)

Report/guidance title	Key features of the report/guidance
Inclusion: Does It Matter Where Pupils Are Taught? (Ofsted 2006a)	This Ofsted report was published in July 2006. It examined the factors that promote good outcomes across a range of different provision for pupils with learning difficulties and disabilities (LDD). It identified the most successful provision as being in additionally resourced mainstream schools where pupils with LDD had the benefit of carefully planned mainstream lessons and small group teaching. The key factors identified by Ofsted for ensuring good progress of pupils with LDD were: involvement of a specialist teacher; good assessment; work tailored to challenge LDD pupils sufficiently; and a commitment from school leaders to ensure good progress for all pupils. Other findings from the HMI report indicated that support from teaching assistants did not ensure good-quality intervention or that adequate progress was made by LDD pupils. A statement of SEN did not determine the quality of provision or outcomes for the LDD pupil in any type of setting. Mainstream and special schools continued to struggle to establish an equal partnership. It stated that the DfES needed to clarify what it meant by 'good progress' for pupils with LDD; local authorities should ensure that children with BESD have full access to thorough assessments and the full range of services; all schools should improve the progress of pupils with LDD by using pupil-level data that are relevant to their age and starting point to ensure that they are suitably challenged; mainstream schools should analyse critically their use and deployment of teaching assistants; and the amount of specialist teaching provided for a range of LDD within a broad and balanced curriculum should be increased in order to develop the knowledge and skills relating to LDD across the school workforce. Ofsted wanted the TDA to improve initial teacher training and continuing professional development for all teachers in the field of LDD.
Government Response to the Education and Skills Committee Report on Special Educational Needs (TSO 2006b)	The government's response to the *Education and Skills Committee's Report on Special Educational Needs* was published in October 2006. The government asked Ofsted to undertake a review of the SEN Framework in 2009 to consider whether or not it is working. In light of that review the government will consider whether the SEN Framework or particular features of it should be reviewed. The government identified five key areas in SEN that it will focus on over the next three years. These are: building capacity in the children's workforce to identify and meet children's needs; promoting a flexible continuum of provision; improving accountability; strengthening the partnerships with parents and children; and improving provision for children with BESD and children with autism. In relation to building capacity in the children's workforce the TDA is working on strengthening the core skills component of ITT and developing new specialist SEN and disability units for the longer three- or four-year ITT courses, as well as developing materials to strengthen these elements during NQT induction. The roll-out of the government's Inclusion Development Programme (IDP) will support the professional development of all teachers. The Education and Inspections Act will endorse the view that the SENCO must be a teacher and a member of the senior leadership team, and clarify the role and responsibilities of the SENCO. The TDA will develop an accredited training system for all newly appointed SENCOs which will become effective from September 2009. In respect of promoting a flexible continuum of SEN provision the government will issue clear guidelines for LAs in relation to local provision. It will also pump-prime funding to support a number of regional centres of excellence. Accountability will be improved by RAISEonline's collection of school performance data, and the extended use of P scales which are to be collected nationally from summer 2007. In relation to strengthening partnerships with parents and children, the government will ensure that parent partnership services have their own budgets, are run by a

Table 1.6 continued

Key reports and government guidance on SEN, disability, inclusion and *Every Child Matters* (*ECM*)

Report/guidance title	Key features of the report/guidance
	management group with independent representation, have links to children's information services and choice advisers, are located away from SEN casework teams, and will be given a voice in local children's services policy development. The government proposes improving BESD capacity through the Inclusion Development Programme (IDP) and the National Programme for Specialist Leaders of Behaviour and Attendance, and by issuing new guidance on meeting the needs of BESD pupils. The government also wishes to strengthen partnerships between mainstream secondary schools and PRUs and special schools to commission their own solutions to tackle behaviour and truancy issues. In relation to autism, the government will improve services for this sector of children and young people, as well as developing a pack for teachers on making effective provision for children with ASD.
Implementing the Disability Discrimination Act (DDA) in Schools and Early Years Settings (DfES 2007c)	This government guidance published in February 2007 comprises DVD and guidance materials designed to help schools, early years settings and local authorities to put into practice the duties of the Disability Discrimination Act (DDA) 1995. It includes an account of how the DDA duties fit with the SEN duties; it incorporates planning duties and provides a clearer definition of disability. There are also case studies which demonstrate how accessibility plans and strategies to make reasonable adjustments in policies and procedures can help to successfully include disabled pupils in all aspects of school life.
The Education of Children and Young People with Behavioural, Emotional and Social Difficulties as a Special Educational Need (DCSF 2008e)	This new DCSF guidance was published in May 2008. The purpose of the guidance was to bring together existing advice on improving achievement, health and emotional well-being for children and young people whose BESD is persistent and provides an obstacle to their learning. The guidance stresses the importance of personalised learning, and developing a whole-school approach to behaviour management such as the SEAL programme for promoting the development of social and emotional skills, positive behaviour, attendance, learning and the mental health of all children. The guidance document indicates that the term covers a wide range of SEN, including children and young people with emotional disorders, conduct disorders and hyperkinetic disorders (including ADD/ADHD) and those whose behavioural difficulties may be less obvious, e.g. those with anxiety, who self-harm, who have school phobia or depression, and those whose behaviour or emotional well-being is seen to be deteriorating. It states that whether a child or young person is considered to have BESD is dependent on a range of factors, including the nature, frequency, persistence, severity and abnormality of the difficulties and their cumulative effect on the child or young person's behaviour, and/or emotional well-being compared with what might generally be expected for a particular age.
How Well New Teachers are Prepared to Teach Pupils with Learning Difficulties and/or Disabilities (Ofsted 2008c)	This Ofsted report was published in September 2008. The report found that of the schools surveyed, few gave new trainees wide enough coverage of learning difficulties in their induction programme, and that as a result new teachers were ill-prepared for meeting the needs of pupils with a wide spectrum of LDD. In relation to initial teacher education (ITE), there were found to be considerable variations in practice and quality across all types and lengths of training in relation to LDD coverage. The most effective ITE linked the teaching of pupils with LDD to other areas of professional studies such as assessment, behaviour management and classroom organisation. It also focused on the implementation of the DDA 1995 in schools, and the development of strategies to support pupils with LDD most commonly found in the classroom. There was a heavy reliance on school placement to provide most of the training for LDD, which varied according to the quality of provision for LDD pupils

Table 1.6 continued

Key reports and government guidance on SEN, disability, inclusion and *Every Child Matters* (*ECM*)

Report/guidance title	Key features of the report/guidance
	within the school. Ofsted identified that it is good practice for NQTs to work alongside the SENCO to help them understand the implications of teaching pupils with LDD. Ofsted made the following recommendations: the TDA should ensure that ITE providers make clear to trainees what a training programme should include if it is to prepare them well to meet the needs of pupils with LDD; ensure that those responsible for monitoring induction provision are fully aware of what constitutes good practice in teaching pupils with LDD; exemplify the professional standards relating to teaching and learning for pupils with LDD. ITE providers should: ensure that a person with appropriate expertise monitors the quality of tuition of pupils with LDD; ensure that a focus on teaching pupils with LDD permeates the course they offer and that the programmes include sessions that deal specifically with the most up-to-date examples of effective practice in this area; emphasise the importance of good leadership and management of the work of other adults to improve the outcomes for pupils with LDD. All training partners should ensure that new teachers are equipped to evaluate how effectively lessons enable pupils with LDD to make good progress. Schools should provide NQTs with sufficient opportunities and a good grounding in the professional standards to prepare them effectively for teaching pupils with LDD. Ofsted also identified the most effective pedagogy relating to LDD that inspectors had observed among new and recently trained teachers. This featured: effective communication with LDD pupils; good understanding of what led to good learning and the ability to adapt their teaching accordingly; clear classroom rules, respect for pupils with LDD and high expectations of their effort and achievement; ability to teach new concepts well to LDD pupils; monitoring the effectiveness of other adults supporting LDD pupils' learning; providing a range of opportunities to enable LDD pupils to take greater responsibility for their own learning.

- The move towards inclusive whole–class teaching in primary schools has meant that teachers find it increasingly difficult to support children with SEN in mainstream primary schools.
- Teacher training for SEN needs to be enhanced and far more practical.
- Overall, there were still tensions existing between competition based on league tables and pupil attainment versus inclusive schooling focusing on the whole child/young person.

It is hoped that the Ofsted HMI review of the SEN framework in 2009 will contribute to any future government revisions of policy and procedures in relation to SEN and inclusion.

Table 1.7

Recent research reports on SEN and inclusion

Research report	Key findings of the research report
Inclusion and Pupil Achievement (Dyson *et al.* 2004)	This DfES report was produced by university researchers commissioned to explore inclusion and its impact on SEN pupil achievement. The key findings were: teachers, parents and LA officers supported the principle of inclusion, but there was less agreement about realising it in practice, or about the impact of inclusion on the achievement of SEN pupils in mainstream schools. Inclusion was found to have positive effects on the wider achievements of all pupils, i.e. social skills and

Table 1.7 continued

Recent research reports on SEN and inclusion

Research report	Key findings of the research report
	understanding. Inclusion could have a negative effect, e.g. having SEN and being included in a mainstream school might be a risk factor for isolation and low esteem. Highly inclusive higher-performing schools adopt a model of provision based on: flexibility of pupil groupings, customisation of provision matched to individual circumstances, careful monitoring of individual pupils alongside whole-school strategies for raising attainment. Lower-performing inclusive schools adopt a similar model. The model is not based on full participation and shared learning experiences by all SEN pupils in common classrooms, and therefore is not fully inclusive, because it features individual, small group or segregated provision where practicable. Schools with higher levels of inclusion tend to be those serving more disadvantaged lower-attaining populations. The researchers found that attainment was largely independent of levels of inclusivity. Therefore schools need not feel anxious about becoming more inclusive, but do need to monitor the effects (both positive and negative) of inclusion developments with care. A shortfall in classroom support, a weakness in teacher skills or managerial planning, or a lack of sufficient funding can affect the inclusion of pupils with SEN in mainstream schools. There was an issue about including BESD pupils in mainstream schools, particularly when their behaviour disrupted lessons and other pupils' learning.
Learning Needs and Difficulties Among Children of Primary School Age: Definition, Identification, Provision and Issues Primary Review Research Briefing 5/2 (Daniels and Porter 2007)	This report 5/2 is one of thirty-two reports in the Primary Review, and was undertaken by researchers from Cambridge University. The research report found that there has been a move away from segregation of SEN pupils towards the integration and inclusion of individual SEN pupils in whole-class teaching, thus broadening the diversity of pupil need. There has been a slowing down in the number of pupils with statements of SEN in the primary phase of education. The children who are obtaining a statement of SEN are those with speech, language and communication needs, autism or BESD. The proportion of children with SEN but no statements has been steadily increasing, particularly in Year 4 among pupils aged 8 to 9 years in the primary sector of education. More boys than girls are identified as having SEN. Children from professional families are more likely to receive support for their SEN than those from working-class families. The attitudes of teachers, parents and pupils are central to developing inclusive practices. The mainstay of support for teachers in primary schools is the SENCO. The approaches to teaching pupils with learning difficulties are not much different from effective practice for all children. However, these LDD pupils do require more opportunities for practice and learning transfer. It is useful for teachers in primary schools to have access to the knowledge that underpins the use of such accommodations in learning in order to inform their teaching practice and their confidence. Teachers need to share this knowledge with teaching assistants and to be effective in managing classroom support. The role of special schools as a resource to support inclusion is underdeveloped, and there is much to be gained from collaborative practice between mainstream and special school staff. Pupils with SEN and BESD are more likely to be excluded from primary school. When pupils with SEN are excluded it slows down the statutory assessment process for obtaining a statement of SEN, and thus exacerbates the child's difficulties. Focusing on evaluating attainment outcomes of SEN pupils can marginalise them even further. The identification of pupils with SEN is resource driven, regulated by statutory guidance which is widely interpreted across LAs. There is uncertain progress towards inclusion in primary schools. Whole-class teaching may be contributing to the higher prevalence of children identified with SEN. Teachers need expertise and support to make adjustments and adaptations to their teaching practices. The researchers from Cambridge University concluded that the

Table 1.7 continued

Recent research reports on SEN and inclusion

Research report	Key findings of the research report
	compatibility and consistency of policy and regulations emanating from the government and its agencies in relation to inclusion should be reviewed, and care should be taken to align these with stated commitments to children with disabilities and difficulties. The tension in current policy of competitive education markets based on school league tables and narrowly conceived measures of pupil attainment on the one hand, and broadly based inclusive schooling within the 'whole child' philosophy, needs to be resolved and reviewed.
SEN: The Truth About Inclusion (Leslie and Skidmore 2008)	This report opens by giving some key statistics relating to SEN and inclusion which illustrate that the government's inclusion policy is in need of an urgent systematic review, with a particular focus on the failures of School Action Plus. Headline statistics reveal that 9,000 special school places have been lost, probably due to the number of statements of SEN issued having fallen by over a third. School Action Plus appears to be replacing the statement of SEN as the number of pupils at this stage has increased greatly. SEN pupils, and particularly those at Action Plus, make up the majority of those excluded, expelled or suspended from school, as well as those with unauthorised or persistent absences from school. These statistics reveal that children's needs are not being met at Action Plus and that the government's inclusion policy is not working. The number of SEN pupils being admitted to PRUs has risen by 70% since 1997, which is high, although PRUs were not designed to admit SEN pupils. The report provides a brief overview of the development of the government's inclusion policy from the Warnock Report in 1978 up to the present time. The Bow Group report concludes that inclusion must be judged by the standard of education and life children receive and not by which building they are educated in. They highlight the concern about the number of SEN children placed in inappropriate schools, i.e. retained in mainstream schools, who would formerly have gone to special schools, and who experience personal isolation and social exclusion. This echoes Warnock's views in *SEN: a New Look* (2005). They finally close the report by clarifying that the unacceptable levels of exclusion of children with SEN from mainstream education, through truancy, exclusion or placement in a PRU, are evidence of the inclusion policy not working. The Bow Group report indicates that a systemic reform must encompass a spectrum of provision to meet a spectrum of needs.
Special Educational Needs and Inclusion (Ellis *et al.* 2008)	This extensive research report undertaken by Canterbury Christ Church University on behalf of the NASUWT investigated: the concepts of inclusion and SEN; teacher attitudes to inclusion; educational policy for inclusion; LA responses to the inclusion agenda; guidance and training for SEN and inclusion to inform classroom practice; and behaviour, SEN and inclusion. The key findings were: there is not a single agreed definition of inclusion. There is some confusion about the meaning and usage of the term SEN among teachers. Medical and social models of SEN coexist, which causes problems for early identification of SEN. Assessment of a special educational need for identifying resource needs (a statement of SEN) is based on learning needs. The ECM agenda brings an increasing emphasis on bio-psycho-social approaches to assessment of SEN through multi-agency working. There is a need for enhanced SEN training for all teachers. The label 'SEN' is limited in allowing teachers to predict and evaluate 'adequate progress'. Teachers have real concerns about the practicalities of inclusion. Teachers' attitudes and values are crucial to the success of inclusion in mainstream schools. Teacher training should offer opportunities for trainees to work with people who have SEN or who are disabled. Training to meet the needs of SEN pupils must be more substantial and reflective for teachers, and build their confidence, competence and preparedness for classroom experiences. Individual

Table 1.7 continued

Recent research reports on SEN and inclusion

Research report	Key findings of the research report
	need since 1997 has been replaced by a SEN policy grounded in school improvement/school effectiveness. The government's strategy for SEN addresses SEN pupil underachievement within the context of the SEN Code of Practice's 'making inadequate progress'. Personalised learning is seen as a means by which to address the dilemma of ensuring positive outcomes for individuals while educating them in group settings. The National Strategies inclusion guidance emphasises a generic strengthening of teaching and learning through 'quality-first teaching' for all pupils. The National Curriculum inclusion statement of principles has established inclusive teaching as a general teaching requirement, and that all teachers are teachers of children with SEN. There are wide variations in LA specialist provision and SEN support service arrangements for including SEN pupils in mainstream schools, which impacts on the day-to-day experience of teachers. More pupils in secondary schools than in primary schools have a statement of SEN. Teachers express concerns about the inclusion of pupils with BESD in mainstream schools. There is a tension existing for teachers between the needs of the BESD pupil and their impact on the needs of other pupils in the inclusive classroom. Teachers need to be proactive in using preventive measures at the low-level disruption stage, so as to stop pupil behaviour escalating into more challenging behaviour.

Useful resources relating to SEND, inclusion and *ECM* policy and legislation

Web-based resources

School Matters – Special Needs: Inclusion is a Teachers TV video which looks at the arguments for and against inclusion. It also features Baroness Warnock speaking about her U-turn in relation to inclusion and pupils with SEN in mainstream schools. It can be downloaded from http://www.teachers.tv/video/3092

Primary Special Needs – Making Inclusion Work is a Teachers TV video which looks at how a mainstream primary school is successfully integrating ten statemented children with varying degrees of disability, which include cerebral palsy and visual impairment. The video can be downloaded from http://www.teachers.tv/video/2861

Secondary Special Needs – Inclusion and Autism is a Teachers TV video which focuses on how a mainstream secondary school is including four boys with autism. The video can be downloaded from http://www.teachers.tv/video/21826

School Matters – Protecting Children – Four True Stories is a Teachers TV video about understanding how teachers and other professionals manage to deal with the challenges raised through child protection issues. It can be downloaded from http://www.teachers.tv/video/5459

School Matters – Every Child Matters is a Teachers TV video which looks at how two inner-city secondary schools are interpreting the *ECM* legislation and some of the difficulties they have faced with its implementation. It can be downloaded from http://www.teachers.tv/video/242

School Matters – Every Child Matters – A Healthcheck is a Teachers TV video which looks at what effect the *Every Child Matters* agenda is having on schools. It also looks at how schools can make *ECM* work effectively. The video can be downloaded from http://www.teachers.tv/video/22378

Special Educational Needs: Linking the Core Standards to Inclusion, SEN and Disability is an excellent online resource from the GTC which looks at how the frameworks and legislation relating to SEN and inclusion link to the core standards for teachers. The resource can be downloaded from http://www.gtce.org.uk/networks/engage home/resources/sen_core_stds

Introduction: Special Educational Needs and/or Disabilities: Undergraduate Primary Materials for ITE is an online TTRB resource, Section 3 of which provides a useful overview of the inclusion statement and Section 6 looks specifically at the key aspects of the Disability Discrimination Act. It can be viewed at http://www.sen.ttrb.ac.uk/viewarticle2.aspx?contentID=15002

Making SENse of CPD is another excellent resource produced by the GTC. It gives a link to many useful organisations relating to SEN. It can be viewed at http://www.gtce.org.uk/networks/connect/resources/sen/

SEN Toolkit is the government's original resource to accompany the SEN Code of Practice. It can be downloaded from http://www.teachernet.gov.uk/wholeschool/sen/teacherlearningassistant/toolkit

Useful publications

DCSF (2007a) *The SEN Statutory Framework*, http://www.standards.dfes.gov.uk/primary/features/inclusion/sen/idp

TDA (2006) *Special Educational Needs in Mainstream Schools. A Guide for the Beginner Teacher*. London: Training and Development Agency for Schools

TDA (2007) *What is Every Child Matters?* London: Training and Development Agency for Schools

Questions for reflection

1 How well do you know and understand the school's/setting's SEN and inclusion policies?

2 How are you implementing SEN and inclusion policies in your practice?

3 How are you ensuring that pupils with disabilities and medical needs are included in lessons and out-of-school-hours activities?

4 What other advice, guidance or information would you welcome about the SEN and Disability Codes of Practice, and where will you seek this from?

5 How are you developing your confidence and knowledge in identifying and meeting the needs of pupils with SEN/LDD?

6 How far do you know how to identify the signs of potential child abuse and follow the correct safeguarding and child protection procedures?

7 How are you contributing to promoting pupils' well-being in relation to the five ECM outcomes?

8 How do you intend to keep up to date with SEND and ECM developments?

9 How far do you agree or disagree that inclusion and ECM are at odds with raising standards?

10 Why might Ofsted's review of the statutory SEN framework be helpful?

CHAPTER 2

Making sense of SEN, disability, inclusion and *ECM*

This chapter will cover:

- Professional and occupational standards for teachers and TAs in relation to making sense of SEN, disability, inclusion and *ECM*
- Identifying barriers to learning and participation
- Meeting a diversity of SEN pupils' needs through personalised learning approaches
- The features of quality-first teaching
- The waves of intervention
- How to make best use of ICT to promote and enhance curriculum access
- Positive approaches to raising pupils' self-esteem
- Meeting pupils' *ECM* well-being across the curriculum and in school
- Useful resources relating to meeting the needs of SEN/LDD pupils
- Further activities

Professional and occupational standards for teachers and TAs in relation to making sense of SEN, disability, inclusion and *ECM*

Table 2.1 outlines the QTS, NQT induction standards and the national occupational standards relevant to teaching assistants in relation to meeting the needs of pupils with SEN and disability.

Identifying barriers to learning and participation

The *SEN Code of Practice* states in relation to identifying barriers to learning:

> It should be recognised that some difficulties in learning may be caused or exacerbated by the school's learning environment or adult/child relationships. This means looking carefully at such matters as classroom organisation, teaching materials, teaching style and differentiation in order to decide how these can be developed so that the child is enabled to learn effectively.

> (DfES 2001c: 44; paragraph 5.6)

Table 2.1

National standards for teachers and TAs related to meeting the needs of pupils with SEN/LDD

QTS standards	Induction standards for NQTs	National occupational standards for TAs
Professional attributes: relationships with children and young people Q1 Have high expectations of children and young people including a commitment to ensuring that they can achieve their full educational potential and to establishing fair, respectful, trusting, supporting and constructive relationships with them.	**1 Developing professional and constructive relationships** C1 Have high expectations of children and young people including a commitment to ensuring that they can achieve their full educational potential and to establishing fair, respectful, trusting, supportive and constructive relationships with them. C38 (a) Manage learners' behaviour constructively by establishing and maintaining a clear and positive framework for discipline, in line with the school's behaviour policy. (b) Use a range of behaviour management techniques and strategies, adapting them as necessary to promote the self-control and independence of learners.	**NVQ Level 2** STL1 Provide support for learning activities, e.g. support teacher planning and the delivery and evaluation of learning activities. STL2 Support children's development, e.g. their social and emotional development. STL6 Support literacy and numeracy activities. STL7 Support the use of ICT for teaching and learning, and prepare ICT resources for teaching and learning. STL8 Use ICT to support pupils' learning and support pupils' use of ICT resources. STL10 Support children's play and learning, particularly their learning through play in early years. STL12 Support a child with disabilities or SEN, e.g. provide care and encouragement; help them to participate in learning activities and experiences. STL13 Contribute to moving and handling individuals, e.g. prepare individual pupils, environments and equipment for moving, handling and repositioning pupils.
Professional knowledge and understanding: teaching and learning Q10 Have a knowledge and understanding of a range of teaching, learning and behaviour management strategies and know how to use and adapt them, including how to personalise learning and provide opportunities for all learners to achieve their potential.		
Achievement and diversity Q19 Knowledge of how to make effective personalised provision for those they teach, including those for whom English is an additional language or who have special educational needs or disabilities, and how to take practical account of diversity and promote equality and inclusion in teaching.	**3 Professional knowledge and understanding:** **(i) Pedagogic practice** C10 Have a good up-to-date working knowledge and understanding of a range of teaching, learning and behaviour management strategies, and know how to use and adapt them, including how to personalise learning to provide opportunities for all learners to achieve their potential. C19 Know how to make effective personalised provision for those they teach, including those for whom English is an additional language or who have special educational needs or disabilities, and how to take practical account of diversity and promote equality and inclusion in their teaching.	**NVQ Level 3** STL18 Support pupils' learning activities and promote independent learning. STL19 Promote positive behaviour, and support pupils in taking responsibility for their learning and behaviour. STL23 Plan, deliver and evaluate teaching and learning activities under the direction of a teacher.
Professional skills: teaching Q25 (a) Use a range of teaching strategies and resources, including e-learning, taking practical account of diversity, and promoting equality and inclusion. (c) adapt their language to		

Table 2.1 continued

National standards for teachers and TAs related to meeting the needs of pupils with SEN/LDD

QTS standards	Induction standards for NQTs	National occupational standards for TAs
suit the learners they teach, introducing new ideas and concepts clearly and using explanations, questions, discussions and plenaries effectively. (d) demonstrate the ability to manage the learning of individuals, groups and whole classes, modifying their teaching to suit the stage of the lesson. **Learning environment** Q31 Establish a clear framework for classroom discipline to manage learners' behaviour constructively and promote their self-control and independence.	**4 Professional skills** **(ii) Teaching** C29 (a) Use an appropriate range of teaching strategies, and resources, including e-learning, which meet learners' needs and take practical account of diversity and promote equality and inclusion. (d) adapt their language to suit the learners they teach, introducing new ideas and concepts clearly, and using explanations, questions, discussions and plenaries effectively. (e) Manage the learning of individuals, groups and whole classes effectively, modifying their teaching appropriately to suit the stage of the lesson and the needs of the learners. C37 (c) Identify and use opportunities to personalise and extend learning through out-of-school contexts where possible making links between in-school learning and learning in out-of-school contexts.	STL25 Support literacy development in relation to reading, writing, speaking and listening skills. STL26 Support numeracy development, i.e. develop numeracy skills and help pupils to use and apply maths. STL27 Support implementation of the early years curriculum, and support teaching and learning activities to deliver the early years curriculum. STL28 Support teaching and learning in a curriculum area. STL31 Prepare and maintain the learning environment. STL33 Provide literacy and numeracy support to enable pupils to access the wider curriculum. STL34 Support gifted and talented pupils, particularly with learning activities. STL37 Contribute to the prevention and management of challenging behaviour in children and young people. STL38 Support children with disabilities or SEN and their families, e.g. contribute to their inclusion and enable them to participate in the full range of activities and experiences. STL39 Support pupils with communication and interaction needs. STL40 Support pupils with cognition and learning needs during learning activities and help them to develop effective learning strategies. STL41 Support pupils with behavioural, emotional and social development needs, e.g. help them to develop positive relationships with

Table 2.1 continued

National standards for teachers and TAs related to meeting the needs of pupils with SEN/LDD

QTS standards	Induction standards for NQTs	National occupational standards for TAs
		others, build their self-esteem, and manage their own behaviour.
		STL42 Support pupils with sensory and/or physical needs, e.g. implement structured learning programmes.
		STL45 Promote children's well-being and resilience, e.g. by helping them to relate to others, and encourage their self-reliance and build their self-esteem.
		STL59 Escort and supervise pupils on educational visits and out-of-school activities.

Source: TDA (2007a, 2007b, 2007c).

Similarly, in *Removing Barriers to Achievement* (2004b) the government also identified barriers to learning:

> Difficulties in learning often arise from an unsuitable environment – inappropriate grouping of pupils, inflexible teaching styles, or inaccessible curriculum materials – as much as from individual children's physical, sensory or cognitive impairments. Children's emotional and mental health needs may also have a significant impact on their ability to make the most of the opportunities in school, as may family circumstances.
>
> (DfES 2004b: 28; paragraph 2.1)

The Excellence in Cities initiative identified a wider range of barriers to learning which were the result of:

- poor literacy and numeracy skills
- underperformance against potential
- English as an additional language
- poor attendance and punctuality
- being a young carer
- long–term sickness
- disaffection
- exclusion from school
- being a victim of bullying
- unstable or difficult family circumstances
- being a looked after child in public care

- several school changes and pupil mobility
- drug- and alcohol-related issues
- the attitude and culture in school.

In addition, the teacher or TA may create barriers to pupils' learning through:

- the language they use to explain a task to pupils;
- the amount the teacher/TA asks a pupil to recall all at once;
- requiring the recording of pupils' ideas to be in writing.

Ofsted in 2004, in relation to the inclusion of pupils with SEN and disability, found that: 'SENCOs in almost half the primary and secondary schools visited identified the perceptions of staff as a major barrier to effective inclusion' (Ofsted 2004: 9; paragraph 29).

Where teachers and TAs have a positive attitude, being sensitive to pupils' individual needs and accepting of diversity, and ensuring that every child and young person can achieve, then they will create a supportive and inclusive barrier-free learning environment.

Ofsted in the same report found that: 'Some pupils with SEN continue to face barriers to participation and achievement, including inaccessible premises and shortfalls in support to reach their potential' (Ofsted 2004: 23; paragraph 108).

The government in *Removing Barriers to Achievement* (2004b) stated that it was committed to removing the barriers to learning that children encountered in school, and that these would be removed through:

- issuing guidance on managing medicines in schools and early years settings;
- producing further training and guidance on disability for early years providers, and a resource bank for schools on how to make reasonable adjustments for disabled pupils;
- promoting better partnership between mainstream and special schools in order to share expertise in SEN;
- encouraging greater use of ICT and e-learning strategies to improve access to education for SEN and disabled children;
- launching a four-year Inclusion Development Programme (IDP) to support schools, early years settings and initial teacher training programmes to enable practitioners/teachers to effectively include children and young people with special educational needs in the following areas: speech, language and communication needs (SLCN) and dyslexia; autistic spectrum disorder (ASD); behavioural, emotional and social difficulties (BESD); and moderate learning difficulties (MLD).

There is a good selection of checklists for identifying barriers to learning and participation within the national primary and secondary strategies SEN and inclusion materials. Figure 2.1 provides a model checklist.

Ofsted , in its report on SEN and disability and inclusive schools (2004), provided a very helpful list of criteria in Appendix B for those teaching and supporting

Aspect	Yes	No
• Teacher and TA have pre-planned together to ensure maximum curriculum access	☐	☐
• Seating of pupils with SEN/LDD has been carefully planned to ensure access	☐	☐
• Appropriate and differentiated learning objectives have been identified and pupils are clear about these	☐	☐
• Pupils are clear about the structure of the school day and lessons, and visual timetables are utilised where appropriate	☐	☐
• New or difficult subject-specific vocabulary is displayed, revisited and clarified	☐	☐
• A check is made to ensure SEN/LDD pupils understand instructions by asking them to explain them back to you in their own words	☐	☐
• Support is in place for those pupils who have difficulty remembering information	☐	☐
• Multi-sensory teaching approaches are used, e.g. VAK (see Table 2.5)	☐	☐
• Pupils are active participants in the lesson/session	☐	☐
• Concrete apparatus and real artefacts are used, including the use of symbols and photographs	☐	☐
• Pre-tutoring is utilised with SEN/LDD pupils to improve their access to the lesson	☐	☐
• Additional supporting adults, such as TAs/LSAs, are effectively deployed throughout the lesson to support learning and pupils' access to learning	☐	☐
• Extra adult support promotes SEN/LDD pupils' independence, protects their self-esteem, and increases their inclusion with their peers	☐	☐
• Pupil buddying is utilised for paired or partner work	☐	☐
• Time out is given to talking partners to enable pupils to share learning ideas and thinking	☐	☐
• The learning environment is emotionally literate, which makes it OK for pupils to make mistakes or take risks in their learning	☐	☐
• A timescale is given by the teacher to differentiate questioning responses, e.g. 3 seconds for pupil responses to closed questions and 10 seconds for open questions	☐	☐
• A range of questions are used in the lesson in a proportion of 50:50 open and closed	☐	☐
• Pupils are encouraged to ask questions	☐	☐
• A distraction-free learning area is provided in the classroom for those pupils who require it, e.g. for those with ASD, BESD	☐	☐
• Classroom rules and routines are displayed and referred to, and these are available in different formats where appropriate	☐	☐
• A variety of pupil groupings is utilised, e.g. whole class, small group, paired work, individual learning, ability groupings, mixed ability groupings, gender groupings	☐	☐
• Tasks and activities are modelled by the teacher/TA/LSA with clear explanations given to pupils	☐	☐
• Scaffolding is utilised to support learning for SEN/LDD pupils as appropriate, e.g. writing frames, clue cards, grids	☐	☐
• Alternatives to written recording are made available for those pupils who need them	☐	☐
• Effective use is made of ICT or augmentive communication technology	☐	☐
• Links are made in learning to pupils' own real-life experiences and current understanding	☐	☐
• Learning is reinforced and transferred by illustrating and emphasising cross-curricular links	☐	☐
• Pupils are given positive, sensitive and constructive feedback if they misunderstand a concept or give an incorrect answer	☐	☐
• Rewards and sanctions are used appropriately for behaviour	☐	☐
• Teaching approaches and curriculum materials reflect cultural diversity	☐	☐
• Tasks, activities and new learning are broken down into smaller steps or chunks for pupils with SEN/LDD	☐	☐

Figure 2.1 Checklist for removing barriers to learning and participation

From Rita Cheminais (2010), *Special Educational Needs for Newly Qualified Teachers and Teaching Assistants*, 2nd edn. London: Routledge. © 2010 Rita Cheminais

SEN/LDD pupils to ensure that barriers to learning and participation were removed in relation to pupil progress, curriculum access, teaching and learning, pupils' positive contributions to the school community, and school policy and practice on inclusion. They did, however, indicate that it was good practice for teachers to use a checklist to identify factors which could prevent the inclusion of pupils with SEN and disability: 'teachers used a checklist during planning sessions to make sure that all the factors which could prevent pupils being included effectively were considered' (Ofsted 2004: 15; paragraph 64). This report can be downloaded from www.ofsted.gov.uk/publications

Meeting a diversity of SEN pupils' needs through personalised learning approaches

Alan Dyson *et al.* in their research commissioned by the DfES on *Teaching Strategies and Approaches for Pupils with Special Educational Needs* (DfES 2004a) found that there was not a distinct SEN pedagogy, as the teaching approaches and strategies used to teach SEN pupils were not sufficiently differentiated from those used to teach all children. This multi-method, inclusive pedagogy approach comprised generic strategies for: raising attainment, promoting active learning, promoting participation and engagement, and responding to personalised learning styles and preferences. However, the research findings did state that it was also important for teachers to have a knowledge of special education and some experience of teaching SEN pupils. It was considered that trainee and newly qualified teachers would gain this knowledge and practical experience from observing the good practice of, and working in partnership with, special school teachers, SEN outreach teachers, ASTs and Excellent Teachers for SEN, and of course the SENCOs' practice within their own setting.

The research report did specify some of the special education knowledge and approaches that were appropriate in relation to: communication and interaction; cognition and learning; behavioural, emotional and social development; and sensory or physical learning needs.

The government in *Raising Barriers to Achievement* commented that: 'Effective teaching for children with SEN shares most of the characteristics of effective teaching for all children. But as schools become more inclusive, so teachers must be able to respond to a wider range of needs in the curriculum' (DfES 2004b: 52; paragraph 3.2).

The government went on to comment: 'We will work collaboratively with the national strategies . . . to further develop the knowledge base and capacity of schools to improve the quality of teaching and learning of children with SEN' (DfES 2004b: 54; paragraph 3.7). This resulted in the launch of the national strategies Inclusion Development Programme (IDP) in 2008, which continued to emphasise a generic strengthening of teaching and learning (quality-first teaching), rather than focusing entirely on specialist approaches. However, the IDP, in its information on removing barriers to learning for each group of SEN, does give some specific strategies relevant to each particular type of SEN.

The IDP is designed to increase the confidence and expertise of primary and secondary school practitioners in meeting high-incidence SEN in mainstream education settings. The programme offers web-based materials which include: teaching and learning resources; practical CPD activities; guidance on effective classroom strategies; models of good practice; and information about sources of more specialist advice.

The IDP will roll out over 2009 and 2010. Current interactive materials related to SLCN, dyslexia and ASD can be viewed and worked through at http://www.standards. dfes.gov.uk/primary/features/inclusion/sen/idp

Personalised learning is emerging as the best approach to take in removing barriers to learning for pupils in mainstream inclusive classrooms. Table 2.2 provides more details about the research into teaching strategies and approaches for pupils with SEN, as well as giving an overview of recent reports and research into personalised learning.

Table 2.3 gives a quick guide for busy teachers and TAs on specific strategies to meet a diversity of additional needs, as part of personalised learning.

What is personalised learning?

Personalised learning is defined by the report of the Teaching and Learning in 2020 Review as: 'Taking a highly structured and responsive approach to each child and young person's learning, in order that they are able to progress, achieve and participate' (Teaching and Learning in 2020 Review Group 2006: 41). In other words, it means tailoring and matching teaching and learning around the way different learners learn in order to meet individual needs, interests and aptitudes so as to enable every pupil to reach their optimum potential.

The government commented:

> We need to provide a personalised education that brings out the best in every child, that builds on their strengths, enables them to develop a love of learning; and helps them to grow into confident and independent citizens, valued for the contribution they make.
>
> (DfES 2004b: 49)

The SEN Code of Practice in 2001 alluded to personalisation in relation to special educational needs: 'Effective management, school ethos and the learning environment, curricular, pastoral and discipline arrangements can help prevent some special educational needs arising and minimise others' (DfES 2001c: 47, 62; paragraphs 5.18 and 6.18).

The government in *Removing Barriers to Achievement* went on to define personalised learning: 'Personalised learning embraces every aspect of school life including teaching and learning strategies, ICT, curriculum choice, organisation and timetabling, assessment arrangements and relationships with the local community' (DfES 2004b: 52; paragraph 3.1).

It also described how teachers could deliver personalised learning by:

- having high expectations of all children
- building on the knowledge, interests and aptitudes of every child
- involving children in their own learning through shared objectives and feedback (assessment for learning)
- helping children to become confident learners

Table 2.2

Research and reports on SEN pedagogy and personalised learning

Research/report title	Key findings of the research/report
Teaching Strategies and Approaches for Pupils with Special Educational Needs: A Scoping Study (DfES 2004a)	This research was commissioned by the DfES. Its key finding was that a combination of teaching strategies (an inclusive pedagogy) was more effective than a single strategy in teaching pupils with a diverse range of SEN. This inclusive pedagogy, which involves multi-method strategies and approaches used for all learners, featured those that:

- raise attainment, e.g. task analysis, target setting with associated guidance, prompts and support, and utilising access strategies to promote cross-curricular learning such as ICT;
- promote active learning by the teacher modelling appropriate learning strategies and developing pupils' thinking skills, reflection and creativity, using investigative and experiential approaches to learning, and access strategies that promote pupils' language development and observational skills, pupil self-assessment and response partner systems; facilitating pupil choice and risk taking in learning; utilising play, drama and simulations, hot seating, role play and making explicit links between learning in and out of school;
- promote participation and engagement, e.g. collaborative and co-operative learning, peer tutoring, real-life problem solving, mentoring, using artists and writers in residence, visiting speakers, sports coaches and work-related learning experiences; using authentic assessment, pupils' opinions and contributions, forging community links;
- responding to personalised learning styles and preferences – visual, auditory and kinaesthetic (VAK) modes of learning, deep learning, multiple intelligences, reflective thinking, active, abstract and concrete thinking; using a SEN pupil's preferred learning style to get new information across and to reinforce more difficult knowledge and concepts; making accommodations to remove barriers to learning for those who have sensory impairments or physical disabilities.

The research found that having a knowledge of special educational needs is an essential component and a key element of pedagogy for teachers. Newly qualified teachers often gain this from special school staff and SEN specialist teachers who share their knowledge, skills and expertise through partnership working and modelling good practice. The report highlighted some key teaching approaches and strategies for the four areas of need as defined by the SEN Code of Practice, but many of these were also featured in the multi-method strategies and approaches.

2020 Vision: Report of the Teaching and Learning in 2020 Review Group (2006)	This report was published in December 2006 and Christine Gilbert chaired the group. It clarified what was meant by the term personalised learning, putting it in the context of the twenty-first century. The report envisaged personalised learning to be about taking a highly structured and responsive approach to each child and young person's learning in order that they progress, achieve and participate. It saw the engagement of pupils and their parents as partners in learning as being important. The report considered that personalised learning helped to narrow the attainment gap existing between different groups of learners. It acknowledged that schools were already responding to personalised learning by ensuring pupils learn how to learn; by using data on pupils' learning for target setting, tracking progress and supporting further achievement; by engaging pupils as active partners with responsibility for participating in designing their learning and providing feedback; using ICT to enhance collaboration and creative learning; using flexible timetabling, increasing curriculum breadth, and greater use of adults other than teachers to extend the range of skills

Table 2.2 continued

Research and reports on SEN pedagogy and personalised learning

Research/report title	Key findings of the research/report
	and support for pupils. The focus of personalised learning according to the report is to: improve the consistency of high-quality teaching to meet learners' needs; and undertake to use wisely whole-class teaching as well as one-to-one, paired and group work. The report recommends building the capacity of teachers and support staff to recognise barriers to learning for children and plan effective intervention, working with other services. It looks at reconfiguring school design and organisation, e.g. changing the traditional school day, enabling 24-hour access to learning via the internet; teaching mixed age groups or pupils of the same attainment levels; having more all-age schools; classrooms designed to support a range of teaching approaches; flexible spaces in schools that can be used for more than one purpose. It acknowledged that personalised learning is an ongoing process of adjustment and improving. It also recognised that the school workforce needs to have the skills important to personalised learning which include: being able to analyse and use data specifically focusing on assessment for learning; understanding how children learn and develop; knowing how to work effectively with others, e.g. parents and professionals from children's services; knowing how to engage pupils as active participants in learning. These skills, the report considered, should be embedded in the learning experience for all trainee and newly qualified teachers.
An Investigation of Personalised Learning Approaches Used by Schools (Seba *et al.* 2007)	This research report commissioned by the DfES on investigating personalised learning approaches focused on: what approaches were being used by schools; how well the approaches used reflected the five key components of personalised learning; identifying the key features of best practice in personalised learning; what additional support schools would welcome in relation to aspects of personalising learning; and how schools were tailoring teaching and learning to meet the needs of specific groups of pupils. The report opens with a definition of personalised learning, clarifying the five key components of this approach. The approaches schools were using to personalise learning for pupils were: reorganisation of teaching assistants and learning mentors to provide more flexible support to individual pupils and small groups; introducing alternative curriculum pathways and work-related learning at Key Stage 4. The five key components of personalised learning were in evidence in schools, but did not have equal emphasis. The key features of best practice in personalised learning were in assessment for learning; pupils taking greater responsibility for their own learning; pupils having genuine pupil voice; strong links with the community; having a flexible curriculum; high levels of pupil and staff participation in learning; learning how to learn. Schools would value additional advice, guidance and support in how to prevent competing interests from limiting personalised learning opportunities, e.g. the standards agenda/league tables and the expansion of vocational work-related opportunities at Key Stage 4. Schools are generally targeting gifted and talented pupils as well as those pupils who fall behind (which includes those with SEN) by extending curricular provision, and through effective deployment of TAs and learning mentors to provide targeted interventions and support. However, there were concerns that pupils of average ability or in the middle may be missed through the adoption of this approach to personalising learning. The report concluded that there was a need for greater clarity and expanded policy guidance on the personalised learning policy in primary schools. There was a tension existing between inclusion and targeting SEN pupils as well as targeting gifted and talented pupils for 'catch-up' and 'stretch'. Further consideration, it was felt, should be given to the role of individual provision within personalised learning.

Table 2.3

Personalised strategies for maximising the achievement of pupils with additional needs

Speech, language and communication needs (SLCN)	Cognition and learning (MLD/SpLD)
<ul><li>Use shorter sentences</li><li>Speak clearly and avoid speaking too quickly</li><li>Pair the pupil up with a good peer language role model and with a supportive group of pupils</li><li>Give the pupil simple messages to take to other pupils or staff (verbal and written)</li><li>Use open questioning giving pupils time to respond</li><li>Read aloud and use commentary to improve pupils' listening skills</li><li>Use discussion and visual cues to support written communication</li><li>Use props to encourage pupils to talk more, e.g. telephone, audio recorders, digital camera/digital video camera</li><li>Engage the pupil in sequencing and matching activities to develop language</li><li>Teach language skills through games, e.g. 20 questions, role play, conversations, guessing games using verbal cues, hot seating</li><li>Provide a quiet area in the classroom for talking and listening activities</li><li>Provide key vocabulary word lists</li><li>Pre-tutor pupil before lesson to familiarise them with new vocabulary</li></ul>	<ul><li>Allow the pupil to work at own pace, giving extra time where needed</li><li>Structure learning into smaller steps, breaking down tasks into smaller components</li><li>Give step-by-step instructions for tasks and write down their homework</li><li>Model what you want the pupil to do</li><li>Provide breaks between tasks</li><li>Support written tasks with mind maps, writing frames, prompt cards, word lists, visual prompts</li><li>Check pupils' understanding by asking them to repeat back what they are to do, or to state three things they have learnt from the lesson</li><li>Allow pupils to present their work in a range of ways other than writing, utilising ICT and multi-media technology</li><li>Utilise a range of multi-sensory teaching and learning approaches (VAK)</li><li>Give immediate positive praise and feedback to reward effort and outcomes</li><li>Provide opportunities for over-learning to consolidate, i.e. peer tutoring</li><li>Give pupils sufficient thinking time to process information</li></ul>
Autistic spectrum disorders (ASD)	**Physical disabilities/sensory impairments**
<ul><li>Give one instruction at a time and ask the pupil to repeat this back</li><li>Use symbols, pictorial instructions, visual timetables</li><li>Introduce one task at a time and provide clear targets</li><li>Give the pupil extra time to process information and complete tasks</li><li>Prepare pupils in advance for any change in classroom or school routines</li><li>Provide a calm, quiet, distraction-free work area in the classroom</li><li>Use simple, consistent language, some closed questions and repetition</li><li>Encourage turn-taking activities and utilise circle time and social stories</li><li>Provide supportive peer partners</li><li>Provide a key adult 'listener' for the pupil</li><li>Make use of the pupils' interests, strengths, talents and skills in teaching activities, wherever possible</li><li>Be very specific, e.g. how many questions or lines of writing you want</li><li>Avoid asking pupils to write about feelings or imaginative experiences</li></ul>	<ul><li>Ensure pupils can see the board, TV or PC monitor clearly</li><li>Dim bright light in the classroom to reduce glare, using window blinds or by reseating the pupil</li><li>Ensure safe movement around the classroom for wheelchair users</li><li>Ensure learning resources are clearly labelled and fully accessible</li><li>Utilise enlarged text where appropriate, or put text on audio tape for visually impaired pupils</li><li>Make use of visual or talking timetables and pre-tutoring</li><li>Produce written information in a range of alternative formats</li><li>Provide extra time for completing tests, examinations or activities</li><li>Take into account that some side effects of medication may cause pupils to be tired, lose concentration and learning capacity, and misbehave</li><li>Ensure that any pupil misunderstandings, misconceptions and mistakes are dealt with sensitively and positively in the classroom</li><li>Use subtitles on TV and video programmes and give written transcripts</li><li>Face hearing-impaired pupils when speaking so they can lip read</li></ul>

Table 2.3 continued

Personalised strategies for maximising the achievement of pupils with additional needs

English as an additional language	Gifted and talented (dual/multiple exceptionality)
• Use plenty of visual clues and real objects • Ensure classroom displays use dual language labelling • Use dual word banks and bilingual dictionaries • Provide collaborative activities that involve talking and role play with peers • Model key language features and structures by demonstration • Provide opportunities for EAL pupils to report back to other peers in the class • Place EAL pupils in supportive groups of peers with good readers and writers who can model English language skills • Provide opportunities for EAL pupils to use their first language, transferring their knowledge to English • Utilise *A Language for All* EAL scale for assessing progress in English language skills	• Set open-ended tasks and utilise open questioning • Provide plenty of opportunities to use multiple intelligences • Develop pupils' higher-order thinking skills, e.g. exploration, reflection, evaluation, prediction, observation • Put extra challenge on learning, e.g. word limits, time limits • Develop their analytical skills, e.g. investigative reporting • Set a quiz question, puzzle, problem or unusual word for the week • Give them a choice on how they present their work and findings • Seek opportunities for cross-phase and cross-key stage working • Provide emotional support, particularly if the pupil is being accelerated into groups with older peers • Give pupils opportunities to work with external experts such as sports coaches, lecturers from university in their specialist area of giftedness or talent

- enabling children to develop the skills they will need beyond school
- inspiring children's learning through passion for their subject
- making the learning experience challenging and enjoyable.

(DfES 2004b: 52–3; paragraphs 3.1, 3.2)

The government published a practical guide to personalised learning in 2008 (DCSF 2008b) which identified a framework comprising nine interrelated features which make up the pedagogy of personalised learning. These nine features are:

- high-quality teaching and learning
- target setting and tracking
- focused assessment
- interventions
- pupil grouping
- the learning environment
- curriculum organisation
- the extended curriculum
- supporting children's wider needs.

Table 2.4 outlines the components of the nine features of the personalised learning framework which make up the personalised learning pedagogy.

Table 2.4

The nine features and components of personalised learning for a personalised pedagogy

Personalised learning feature	Components of effective practice
1 High-quality teaching and learning	a) designing highly focused teaching sequences/lesson plans for the high demands of pupil engagement b) designing reasonable adjustments and special educational provision with lesson plans c) focusing on questioning, modelling and explaining d) promoting pupil talk e) supporting pupil independence and their learning
2 Target setting and tracking	a) translating National Curriculum, P scale, GCSE/Diploma targets into curricular targets b) using pupil-level progress data to identify those pupils and groups who are off target, falling behind, underachieving c) adjusting teaching and intervention programmes in light of the tracking information d) providing regular feedback to pupils and their parents/carers
3 Focused assessment	a) incorporating learning objectives, learning outcomes and success criteria into daily practice b) supporting pupils in assessing and evaluating their learning through peer and self-assessment c) using assessing pupil progress (APP) as a central part of periodic assessment
4 Interventions	a) linking learning developed in intervention programmes into mainstream lessons b) incorporating individual tuition into the overall approach to intervention c) evaluating the quality and impact of current intervention programmes
5 Pupil grouping	a) evaluating the impact of class teaching and particular groupings, e.g. mixed ability, ability sets, gender groups b) incorporating a rapid range of pupil grouping options (whole class, small group, pairs) in lessons c) developing guided learning as an integral part of lesson organisation
6 The learning environment	a) adapting the organisation of the classroom/learning environment to the pupils' learning needs b) developing the use of learning resources and particularly ICT c) ensuring ICT is used to support access for disabled pupils and those with SEN d) making effective use of the outdoor learning environment as an extension of classroom-based learning
7 Curriculum organisation	a) choosing an overall curriculum model/structure that caters for the needs of all pupils b) providing specific support for certain groups, of pupils, including pupils with SEN, disability, EAL, and the gifted and talented c) incorporating flexibility into curriculum organisation and delivery to ensure greater coherence from the pupils' perspective

Table 2.4 continued

The nine features and components of personalised learning for a personalised pedagogy

Personalised learning feature	Components of effective practice
8 The extended curriculum	a) offering a range of 'out-of-hours' activities which enhance and extend the basic curriculum b) ensuring access for all groups of pupils to extended curriculum activities c) involving parents/carers as well as the wider community in extended provision d) providing access to other services/practitioners, including health and social services
9 Supporting pupils' wider needs	a) maintaining close communication with parents/carers b) developing multi-agency links and active multi-professional partnerships to support vulnerable pupils c) developing the role of the personal tutor/key adult as a first point of contact for parents/carers

Source: DCSF (2008b: 54–5).

The features of quality-first teaching

All children and young people have an entitlement to access quality-first teaching (QFT) as part of personalised learning at Wave 1 intervention, within a whole-school/whole-class learning context.

Quality-first teaching consists of the day-to-day interactions between a teacher and their pupils known as pedagogy, that seeks to engage and support the learning of all children and young people in the inclusive classroom. It builds on pupils' prior learning, and responds appropriately to pupil voice and pupil diversity.

Quality-first teaching differentiates the curriculum by staging work by level of support, by open-tasking, i.e. setting mixed ability tasks that challenge at every level, and by extension or enhancement activities. This approach lends itself to planning for making reasonable adjustments for disabled learners and provision for SEN pupils. Differentiation as part of quality-first teaching is also about responding to pupils' interests, preferences or priorities in learning, i.e. offering options between topics or texts.

Differentiation is also synonymous with inclusion. It builds on pupils' past achievement and provides challenge for further achievement and opportunities for successful learning. Differentiation can be done by:

Content/task – a range of different activities is set to match different abilities.

Interest – activities are given that relate to pupils' interests.

Pace – time limits or deadlines for task completion are set.

Level – parallel graduated curriculum materials are used for the same subject area.

Access/resources – pupils carry out similar activities but use modified or additional materials and learning aids.

Response – pupils record learning outcomes in a range of different ways.

Depth/sequence – pupils follow a common topic but study and develop different aspects of the topic further, e.g. the Second World War – food, fashion, leisure, family life.

Structure – the curriculum is delivered to some pupils in smaller steps, while other pupils receive a section or unit all at once.

Support – the teacher or TA/LSA may give more individual time and attention to certain pupils, e.g. pupils with SEN/LDD, gifted and talented pupils, EAL pupils.

Teaching style – the teacher uses a wider range of teaching approaches in a lesson, e.g. VAK.

Grouping – pupils work independently, in pairs, in small groups or as a whole-class group for particular activities.

Quality-first teaching builds upon children's and young people's progression in learning. It is designed to move learners from where they are to where they need to be in relation to expectations. Quality-first teaching draws on a repertoire of teaching strategies and techniques that are closely matched to the specific learning objectives and the particular needs of the pupils in a class group. (Table 2.5 illustrates the repertoire of teaching strategies and learning styles.)

Quality-first teaching demands full pupil participation and sets high but realistic challenges. It encourages pupils to talk about learning and fosters behaviour for learning. Quality-first teaching adopts guided learning/work for small groups integrated into whole-class teaching: work is pitched at appropriate levels for differing groups within the class, thus enabling the teacher to give closer attention to pupils and intervene and challenge them in a sustained, proactive and fair way.

In developing quality-first teaching, schools pay particular attention to the development of strategies like questioning, modelling, thinking aloud and explaining to advance pupils' learning. These approaches are adjusted to recognise the skills, interests and prior learning of individual pupils.

How to plan for quality-first teaching

Effective planning and lesson design make the starting point for quality-first teaching and learning. The flow chart (Figure 2.2) which illustrates an effective planning model needs to be supported by the primary or secondary curriculum frameworks.

The characteristics and features of quality-first teaching include:

- highly focused lesson design with sharp objectives, differentiated and personalised to match learners' needs, e.g. planning to make reasonable adjustments for pupils with learning difficulties and disabilities;

- high levels of interaction for all pupils, including those with SEN/LDD;

- high amounts of pupil involvement and engagement with their learning;

- appropriate use of teacher questioning, modelling and explanation;

- emphasis on co-operative learning and thorough dialogue, with regular opportunities for pupils to talk in pairs, individually and in groups;

- an expectation that pupils will accept responsibility for their own learning and work independently;

Table 2.5

Teaching and learning styles as part of quality-first teaching

Auditory	Logical/theorist
Characteristics	**Characteristics**
Good listeners; fluent, expressive talkers; good vocabulary; explains things clearly to others; enjoys brainstorming; quick to learn from listening to others; self-talks; thinks aloud	Enjoys knowing and applying theories, concepts, models, principles; likes logical explanations; enjoys estimating, problem solving, doing quizzes and puzzles; works through tasks in an orderly and methodical way. Can identify connecting links
Learns least when:	**Learns least when:**
Unclear guidance on how to do a task is given or when lengthy descriptions are given	Feelings or emotions are involved, or tasks are ambiguous and unstructured, or they are 'put on the spot'
Appropriate teaching approaches	**Appropriate teaching approaches**
Use audio tape activities; provide opportunities to discuss in groups; give opportunity for oral feedback; use investigative reporting and interviewing; give opportunities for pupils to express ideas in their own words	Provide step-by-step plans/instructions; use data in a variety of forms; provide a theory or principle to work from; give them time to explore ideas and think things through
Visual	**Kinaesthetic/activist**
Characteristics	**Characteristics**
Observant; quick to see things others miss; photographic memory; good sense of direction; good imagination	Enjoys teamwork; doing practical activities; has good co-ordination and manual dexterity; enjoys concrete experiences; learns by example, demonstration, modelling; remembers by doing; fidgets; easily distracted; impulsive
Learns least when:	**Learns least when:**
Under time constraints or when they cannot see any relevance in the task	Passive, or when work is solitary, or asked to attend to theory or detail
Appropriate teaching approaches	**Appropriate teaching approaches**
Need time to watch and think things through; respond best to visual materials, video and websites; introduce flow charts and diagrams, mind maps, and brainstorming; utilise picture sequencing; visualisation exercises; highlighting text; drawing to demonstrate their understanding of a text	Provide opportunities to touch/manipulate objects; build models, participate in activity-based learning; investigation/experimental work

- regular use of encouragement and authentic praise to engage and motivate pupils;
- high expectations for all pupils which take into account age–related expectations, individual differences and needs;
- clarity of learners about expected learning outcomes and the learning objectives;
- learning that builds and scaffolds on prior knowledge and understanding;
- links made to learning elsewhere across the curriculum or in intervention groups to promote transfer of knowledge, skills and understanding;
- use of a range of multi–sensory teaching approaches which are modelled by the teacher and teaching assistant;

1   Locating the teaching sequence or lesson in the context of:

- the scheme of work

- the pupils' prior knowledge and understanding

2   Identifying the learning objectives for the pupils

3   Structuring the teaching sequence/lesson as a series of episodes by separating the learning into distinct stages/steps and selecting:

- the best pedagogic approach to meet the learning objectives

- the most appropriate teaching and learning strategies and techniques

- the most effective organisation for each episode

4   Ensuring coherence by providing:

- a stimulating start to the lesson that relates to the objectives

- transitions between episodes which are clearly signposted for pupils

- a final plenary that reviews learning and identifies next steps

DCSF (2008b: 11).

Figure 2.2 Effective planning model for a lesson

- access to ICT and multi-media technology to enhance and promote curriculum access and learning outcomes;

- learners build up their own repertoire of learning skills;

- stimulating and inspiring classroom/learning environment with informative interactive displays on classroom walls;

- opportunities for pupils throughout and at the end of the lesson to review and reflect upon their own learning and progress;

- behaviour for learning is fostered through the use of positive approaches, i.e. pupil buddies, SEAL;

- effective deployment of TAs/LSAs to promote inclusion and independent learning (DCSF 2008b: 12).

Ofsted, in its report *Special Educational Needs and Disability: Towards Inclusive Schools* (2004), identified the features of inclusive quality-first teaching for pupils with SEN/LDD:

- effective teamwork among teachers and teaching assistants;
- specially devised/adapted materials and methods of teaching tailored well to pupils' needs;
- activities capturing pupils' interest and participation;
- careful grouping of SEN pupils to ensure productive working with others;
- staff showing positive attitudes and having high expectations of SEN pupils;
- adequate support for ICT;
- multi-sensory resources in all parts of lessons;
- personal targets incorporated into the learning objectives;
- opportunities for independent learning;
- next steps in learning carefully spelled out.

(Ofsted 2004: 15; paragraphs 63, 64)

Inclusive classroom practice for pupils with SEN/LDD

Inclusive classroom practice is synonymous with quality-first teaching and personalised learning. It is informed by the National Curriculum statutory inclusion statement of principles.

Ofsted (2004) identified the features of effective inclusive practice in mainstream schools:

- a climate of acceptance of all pupils, including those who have distinctive needs;
- careful preparation of placements, covering the pupils with SEN, their peers in school, parents and staff;
- the availability of sufficient suitable teaching and personal support;
- widespread awareness among staff of the particular needs of pupils with significant special needs and an understanding of practical ways of meeting them in classrooms and elsewhere;
- sensitive allocation to teaching groups and careful modification of the curriculum, timetables and social arrangements;
- the availability of appropriate materials and teaching aids and adapted accommodation;
- an active approach to personal and social development, as well as to learning, especially to lessen the effects of the divergence of social interests between older pupils with SLD, and sometimes those with ASD, and their peers;
- well-defined and consistently applied approaches to managing difficult behaviour;
- assessment, recording and reporting procedures which can enhance and express adequately the progress of pupils who may make only small gains in learning and personal development;
- involving parents as fully as possible in decision making, keeping them well informed about their child's progress and giving them as much practical support as possible;
- developing and taking advantage of training opportunities, including links with special schools and other schools providing for a similar group of pupils with SEN.

(Ofsted 2004: 19; paragraph 82)

Table 2.6

Characteristics of an inclusive early years/school setting

- Members of the community use the extended services
- Teamwork is a strength and staff are responsive to children's needs
- The building is accessible to wheelchair users
- Protected quality time is made available for staff and external practitioners to reflect upon and discuss their practice and interventions together
- Strong links are established between the setting and the community
- Effective use is made of the local authority children's services
- Ongoing professional development opportunities for staff in relation to inclusion and *Every Child Matters* are available
- A key adult/worker system is in place for every child
- The SENCO/*ECM* manager has sufficient time to carry out their role
- Displays around the setting reflect cultural diversity
- Guidance is available to staff on choosing culturally diverse resources
- Effective transition arrangements are in place for pupils
- Whole school/setting planning is governed by the needs of the children
- Pupil voice is valued and they participate in decision making
- Parents'/carers' views are valued and they are made to feel welcome
- Effective policies are in place for inclusion and equal opportunities
- The setting uses a range of formats for communicating with parents/carers and members of the local community
- The main entrance to the setting is welcoming, with a helpful receptionist

Table 2.6 provides a useful list of how to recognise whether an early years setting or school is inclusive. It takes a holistic whole-school approach, which it is important to identify if as a newly qualified teacher or TA you are seeking a job in an educational setting.

The waves of intervention

The National Strategies refer to the waves of intervention which provide an inclusive model and approach to teaching and additional interventions, designed to minimise underachievement and close the attainment gap between particular groups of learners. The waves of intervention sit alongside personalisation and the graduated response of the *SEN Code of Practice*.

Wave 1 = quality-first teaching (QFT)

This wave features high-quality, inclusive teaching to meet the needs of all learners, based on their prior learning. It is focused on moving all learners from their current starting point/current attainment to where they need to be and should be, and relies on making effective use of pupil-level attainment and well-being data in order to do so.

Quality-first teaching is an entitlement for all children at all stages of the *SEN Code of Practice*. It is also related to the social and emotional aspects of learning (SEAL) at the primary and secondary phases.

Wave 2 = quality-first teaching plus additional, time-limited, tailored intervention support programmes

This wave of interventions is designed to increase the rates of progress and secure learning for groups of learners to put them back on course to meet or exceed national expectations. This usually takes the form of a tight, structured programme of small-group support which is carefully targeted and delivered by TAs or teachers. This support can occur outside and in addition to whole-class lessons, or be built into mainstream lessons as part of guided work. Intervention support helps children and young people to apply their learning in mainstream lessons, and ensures that motivation and progress in learning are sustained. It also applies to interventions for children and young people who need additional help in developing emotional, social and behavioural skills. Examples of Wave 2 interventions are ELS, ALS, FLS and Springboard Maths to support 'catch-up'.

Wave 3 = quality-first teaching plus increasingly individualised intervention programmes, based on independent evidence of what works

Expectations are to accelerate and maximise progress and to minimise performance gaps. This may involve specialist teacher support or inputs from a highly trained TA/LSA delivered one to one or to a small group to support SEN pupils towards the achievement of very specific targets. Wave 3 focused and structured interventions align with the *SEN Code of Practice* graduated response at Action, Action Plus and a statement of SEN. Wave 3 interventions are more effective when they operate intensively over a short, focused period of up to twenty weeks. Ideally, pupils on Wave 3 interventions should make on average at least twice the normal rate of progress. Examples of Wave 3 interventions include Reading Recovery, Toe-by-Toe, Phono-Graphix programmes and multi-sensory programmes for pupils with specific learning difficulties.

How to make best use of ICT to promote and enhance curriculum access

The DfEE, in *Excellence for All Children: Meeting Special Educational Needs* (1997), commented: 'ICT should be used to give children with special educational needs maximum access to the curriculum and to help them reach their learning potential' (DfEE 1997: paragraph 1:30). Similarly, the National Curriculum teaching requirements on the use of ICT across the curriculum states that: 'All pupils should be given opportunities to apply and develop their ICT capability through the use of ICT tools to support their learning in all subjects' (http://www.nc.uk.net/use_ict.html).

ICT, as part of making reasonable adjustments to promote and enhance curriculum access, enables pupils with special educational needs and disabilities not to be put at a disadvantage in relation to their learning. ICT, as one of the important features of personalised learning in the inclusive classroom, is an essential tool to enable SEN/LDD pupils to gain some level of independence in their learning. Table 2.7 illustrates how ICT can be used for specific groups of SEN/LDD pupils.

BECTA produces an excellent free downloadable guide to schools on how to make software accessible to pupils with SEN. It is available from http://publications.becta.org.uk/display.cfm?resID=32113

Table 2.7

Benefits and use of ICT with SEN/LDD pupils

Nature of SEN/LDD	Example of ICT resources	Benefits of using the ICT resources
Physical disabilities and sensory impairments	Assistive technology: touch screens, switches, head- and eye-operated systems, high-visibility cursor, adapted mice, rollerball, joystick, keyguards, concept keyboard, overlay keyboards, speech feedback, screen magnifiers, screen readers, electronic braillers, big pointer utilities	• Provides switch access for tasks such as matching, sorting, sequencing, word processing • Translates text into speech and speech into text • Enables written work/text to be enlarged, produced in coloured font and incorporating symbols
Cognition and learning difficulties	Spell and grammar checkers, talking books, drill and practice software programs, sound and graphics facilities, CD-ROMs, talking word processors, work list facilities	• Software programs matched and tailored to pupils' ability • Provides a structured clutter-free working environment • Enhances study skills such as scanning text, summarising, researching internet • Enables pupils to consolidate their learning through skill practice and repetition • Offers e-learning opportunities • Offers a multi-sensory learning approach • Offers differentiated learning activities with different levels of challenge • Offers information in a range of different ways
Behavioural, emotional and social difficulties	Educational games software, multi-media programmes, animations in software programs, digital camera, digital video camera	• Helps BESD pupils to improve their concentration • Offers a non-judgemental and non-threatening learning situation • Motivates pupils, offering them opportunities to experience success in learning • Enables pupils to take greater responsibility for their own learning • Enables pupils to work on tasks that are more manageable and achievable • Enables the BESD pupils to be more confident in taking risks in their learning • Provides social interaction opportunities for undertaking computer work with peers • Raises self-esteem by enabling pupils to produce quality written work • Helps to develop language and social skills

Improving access to ICT for pupils with SEN/LDD

Here are some basic tips to help you assess your classroom or learning support area, in order to ensure SEN/LDD pupils are able to access ICT hardware.

● Ensure computer monitor screens do not directly face windows where bright light reflection or glare which disturbs screen viewing can occur.

● Ensure the computer monitor screen is at least 17 inches or larger in size.

● Ensure the workstation level is appropriate to enable any pupils in wheelchairs to use the computer comfortably.

● Check whether the computer keyboard needs to be tilted at an angle.

● Use the options available on the computer control panel to improve access, e.g. to set up sticky keys, filter keys or toggle keys or change the mouse properties.

● Obtain additional adaptations to computer hardware if the pupil has poor motor control, e.g. a key guard, big keys, roller ball, larger-sized mouse, a joystick or a touch pad control in place of a conventional mouse.

● Seek further advice and guidance from the local authority ICT consultant.

Computer software resources to support SEN/LDD pupils' learning

There is a good range of computer software programs available to support and reinforce SEN/LDD pupils' learning. Your school SENCO, local authority ICT consultant or special school ICT co-ordinator will all be able to provide further advice on which software to use. Table 2.8 provides an overview of a sample of the most popular packages used in mainstream settings.

Three helpful websites on ICT resources for SEN/LDD pupils which offer a good range of ICT software and hardware packages are: http://www.inclusive.co.uk/index. shtml; http://www.onestopeducation.co.uk/; http://www.becta.org.uk/inclusion/

Teachers TV has a very good video which shows how to use ICT in the primary school classroom to enable pupils, including those with SEN, to produce an electronic storybook (e-book). It can be viewed or downloaded from: http://www.teachers.tv/node%252F5415

There is also a useful document on ICT and the *Every Child Matters* outcomes available from the website http://www.ictineducation.org

Positive approaches to raising pupils' self-esteem

Self-esteem refers to the way individuals see themselves, think and feel about themselves or judge their self-worth (Table 2.9). It is also about how they think others feel about them or perceive them. Low self-esteem affects pupils' capacity to learn as it causes a barrier to learning. Low self-esteem is often evident in pupils with BESD.

The causes of low self-esteem

Low self-esteem in pupils may be a result of their:

● feeling that they don't fit in with their peer group, or don't live up to media images of how young people should be;

● need to adjust to adolescence;

● striving for independence from their parents in front of their peers/friends;

Table 2.8

A sample of ICT software programs for pupils with SEN/LDD

Name of ICT software	Description of software package
Wordshark 4	This program combines computer games with learning to read and write. Sound graphics are used as well as text to teach SEN pupils word recognition and spelling. It incorporates letters and sounds to complement the national strategies initiative. This software package is available from White Space.
Numbershark 4	This program provides a range of mathematical games for SEN pupils, which covers the four rules of numbers, decimals, fractions and percentages. This software package is available from White Space.
Clicker Plus	Clicker Plus provides an on-screen keyboard with speech to make writing easier. There is another version called Switch Clicker which is for pupils with SEN who are unable to use a mouse or a keyboard.
Clicker 4	Clicker 4, Find Out and Write About, Planet Wobble are all software programs that focus on developing literacy skills, multi-media, access and communication.
Write Online	Write Online offers word prediction, word banks and writing frames and uses integrated speech.
Write: Outloud	All these software programs are available from Crick Software.
Co:Writer	These software programs by Don Johnston Special Needs Limited provide high-quality ICT intervention resources to enable SEN pupils to acquire literacy skills. They offer reading, writing, word-study and computer access products.
Penfriend	This is a software writing package by Penfriend Limited which is designed specifically to help pupils with dyslexia or those who are physically disabled. It predicts the next word the pupil intends to type, it speaks as pupils type, and it offers an on-screen keyboard and it can read back documents, pupils' own work and web pages.
Writing with symbols	This software supports pupils with SEN in relation to writing. It enables the pupil to select letters, words or images. The program is available from Widgit Software.
Talking Write Away	This is a talking educational word processor that enables the pupil to hear their work being spoken. It is available from Black Cat.

- worrying that they don't have the right skills for undertaking an activity;
- feeling they can never live up to their parents' or others' expectations.

Strategies for raising pupils' self-esteem

- Encourage pupils to adopt a 'can–do' approach.
- Give praise and recognition to counter pupils' negative feelings.
- Give the pupil a responsibility to make them feel valued.
- Focus on the pupil's strengths and talents.
- Offer reassurance and encouragement.
- Build success into every day for the pupil.
- Act as a positive role model for good self–esteem.
- Show pupils that you can sometimes make mistakes.
- Use positive affirmations and language.

Table 2.9

Characteristics of low and high self-esteem

Low self-esteem characteristics	High self-esteem characteristics
Difficulty expressing themselves	Like themselves
Fear rejection by friends/family	Know themselves well
Reluctant to complete work for fear of failure	Willing to learn from their mistakes
Tell lies to mask their failings	Kind to themselves and others
Defensive to hide weaknesses	Stand up for themselves
Blame others for their failings	Make amends if hurt others' feelings
Seek constant reassurance	Accept the choices they make

- Ensure peers show respect for the pupil's thoughts and efforts.
- Teach the pupil to cope with disappointments or failures.
- Prepare the pupil for new experiences or changes in routines.
- Help the pupil to set themselves goals or targets to make them feel better about themselves.

Developing emotional literacy within the classroom

Emotional literacy, also referred to as emotional intelligence, is the ability to recognise, understand, manage and appropriately express emotions. It is about managing yourself and your emotions and understanding and interpreting the emotions and feelings of others.

Developing emotional literacy among pupils within the classroom is important because emotions influence motivation, concentration, creativity, behaviour, learning, memory and achievement. Knowing how to interpret and manage emotions also contributes to pupils' well-being.

Emotional literacy influences a pupil's self-esteem. If pupils feel good about themselves, then they will learn more efficiently, and be happier and more co-operative. A pupil who is angry or anxious will not learn as effectively.

Strategies for developing pupils' emotional literacy

When the teacher or teaching assistant understands pupils' feelings, good adult/pupil relationships become easier to establish. Trainee or newly qualified teachers or teaching assistants can develop emotional literacy in pupils by:

- creating situations involving successful social interactions to help build pupils' self-esteem and develop their positive thinking;
- designing activities where pupils have to work together co-operatively, and debriefing them on the nature of the co-operative skills they have used;
- modelling effective social behaviour for pupils and encouraging them to talk about this and how they might feel in hypothetical situations;
- using social stories to help pupils develop an understanding about feelings and emotions;
- encouraging pupils to talk through on a one-to-one basis with you why something is bothering them;
- listening with empathy to understand how pupils are feeling;

- articulating your feelings within the classroom;

- asking pupils to share their feelings about a subject or topic;

- allowing pupils to put their feelings on post-it notes and post them in a box in the classroom anonymously if they are unwilling to share feelings openly;

- using role play and drama activities to enable pupils to express their emotions and feelings;

- incorporating circle time into the weekly class routine to give pupils the opportunity to explore feelings and share emotions together in a safe emotionally literate environment.

Positive approaches to managing pupil behaviour: what do we mean by behavioural, emotional and social difficulties?

Pupils with behavioural, emotional and social difficulties (BESD) will have a continuum of persistent difficulties, irrespective of ability. These are likely to include: being withdrawn or isolated; showing disruptive, hyperactive or challenging behaviour; lacking concentration; seeming depressed; having eating disorders or conduct disorders such as oppositional defiance disorder (ODD), attention deficit disorder (ADD) and attention deficit hyperactivity disorder (ADHD) or having Tourette's Syndrome.

Why do pupils have behavioural difficulties?

Pupils may have behavioural difficulties for any or all of the following reasons:

family circumstances: due to child abuse, neglect or deprivation; family break-up such as parents divorcing or separating; family illness or bereavement;

within-child factors: due to a lack of self-confidence, low self-esteem, poor social skills, sensory/physical impairment, specific learning difficulties, tiredness;

school factors: due to an inappropriate curriculum offer, ineffective rewards system, inflexible timetabling, ineffective whole-school behaviour policy which is not implemented consistently;

classroom factors: due to a mismatch between curriculum delivery and pupils' learning styles, lessons being too long, insufficient curriculum differentiation, insufficient challenge in learning activities, unclear teacher instructions or explanations, poorly planned lessons, didactic teaching, little pupil participation in learning, inappropriate pupil groupings or seating arrangements in the classroom.

Different levels of behaviour in the classroom

The school's behaviour policy should indicate and clarify what are considered to be minor and serious behaviour problems. Table 2.11 provides a quick guide.

The ABC of behaviour management

The ABC is a useful approach to use in recording and analysing significant pupil behavioural incidents. **A** refers to the **A**ntecedents, i.e. the events leading up to or happening before the behaviour occurs. **B** refers to the actual **B**ehaviour that occurs. **C** refers to the **C**onsequences, i.e. what happens after the behaviour; for example, how the pupil who misbehaved feels, how others react to the pupil behaviour (other pupils

Table 2.10

Minor and serious behaviour problems

Minor behaviour problems	Serious behaviour problems
Calling out	Swearing
Being off task	Destroying other pupils' work
Being out of seat in class	Making sexual/racial comments
Throwing and flicking objects, paper	Vandalising books and equipment
Distracting other peers from their work	Violent, dangerous behaviour
Arriving late for lessons	Bullying
Being cheeky	Fighting
Talking when the teacher is talking	Walking out of class and school
Not listening to the teacher	Persistent lying
Forgetting to bring books/equipment	Bringing offensive weapons to school

and staff). Figure 2.3 provides a template for recording an ABC of a significant behaviour incident.

The basic rules for behaviour management

The four Rs framework is a practical approach for managing behaviour used in teaching assistants' national training. The four Rs are rights, rules, routines and responsibilities. Table 2.11 gives an outline of the framework, and teachers as well as teaching assistants will find it useful. It also helps to inform a classroom code of conduct for establishing behaviour for learning among pupils.

Figure 2.4 offers a tracking record for an individual pupil's behaviour over a day. This model can be adapted and customised to cover a week's lessons.

Twenty top tips for managing pupil behaviour

1 Condemn the behaviour and not the pupil.

2 Reprimand the pupil privately rather than publicly.

3 Listen to the pupil's reason and explanation for their behaviour.

4 Deal with the behaviour calmly and quietly to minimise disruption.

5 Catch the pupil being good, using positive praise to reinforce good behaviour.

6 Avoid confrontation and defuse it with humour or by changing the subject.

7 Refer the pupil regularly to the classroom rules which are phrased positively.

8 Use non-verbal cues, e.g. a look, raised eyebrows, being silent, making eye contact, using symbols.

9 Give the pupil a job to do or a message to take.

10 Provide time out and a quiet area in the classroom where the pupil can cool off, calm down.

11 Teach the pupil to use anger management techniques, e.g. count to ten, squeeze a stress ball, do some deep breathing, sit on their hands.

12 Ensure tasks are matched to pupil ablility.

13 Pair the pupil up with a peer who is a good role model for behaviour.

14 Make explicit to the pupil the consequences of their misbehaviour.

Pupil name: _____

Date and place of incident: _____

Antecedents:

Behaviour:

Consequences:

Figure 2.3 ABC template to record a significant behaviour incident

From Rita Cheminais (2010), *Special Educational Needs for Newly Qualified Teachers and Teaching Assistants*, 2nd edn. London: Routledge. © 2010 Rita Cheminais

Table 2.11

The four Rs framework for behaviour management

Rights	Routines
The rights of all pupils in the class to: ● learn ● be safe (physically and emotionally) ● have dignity and respect The right of every teacher/teaching assistant to: ● teach and provide support for learning	Daily routines must be followed consistently when: ● entering and leaving the classroom ● getting out work and putting work away ● moving around the classroom ● asking and answering questions ● going to use the computer or visit the school library ● going into and out from a school assembly
Rules	**Responsibilities**
There are three basic rules that all pupils must follow: ● follow the teacher's/TA's directions and instructions ● keep hands, feet and objects to themselves ● no swearing, name calling or put-downs	Helping pupils to take greater responsibility for their own behaviour involves using the language of choice. For example: 'If you choose not to settle down to your work then you will be choosing to stay in at break/playtime to finish it.' 'I need you to choose to put that magazine away and go back to your place.' 'Thank you for choosing to sit away from Peter and to get on with your work.'

15 Apply sanctions for misbehaviour fairly and consistently.

16 Introduce breaks from task or vary tasks to prevent boredom which can lead to misbehaviour, e.g. brain breaks and brain exercises.

17 Seat the pupil in front of the teacher at the front of the class.

18 Ensure the pupil can succeed at something in the lesson or during the day.

19 Use the pupil's home–school diary to keep parents informed about their child's behaviour – positive and negative aspects.

20 When a pupil's behaviour is dangerous or may compromise the safety of other pupils in the class, move the pupil out of the classroom and call for a senior member of staff to deal with the pupil's behaviour.

Meeting pupils' *ECM* well-being across the curriculum and in school

The Education and Inspections Act 2006, which became effective from September 2007, placed a duty on all maintained primary, secondary and special schools, PRUs and academies to promote the well-being of pupils.

The five *ECM* outcomes are at the heart of everything a school does and are fundamental to, and reinforced through, its curriculum. The QCA has published an excellent document entitled *Every Child Matters at the Heart of the Curriculum* (2008).

This can be downloaded at: www.qca.org.uk/qca_15949.aspx

Table 2.12 provides an overview of how the *ECM* outcomes are included across the curriculum. It should assist teacher planning.

Pupil name: _____ Date: _____

Nature of the pupil's classroom behaviour (Put a tick in the relevant lesson box if the feature was present)	Lesson 1	Lesson 2	Lesson 3	Lesson 4
Arrived to the lesson on time	☐	☐	☐	☐
Arrived to the lesson late	☐	☐	☐	☐
Settled down quickly to work	☐	☐	☐	☐
Took some time to settle down to work	☐	☐	☐	☐
Brought the correct books and equipment to the lesson	☐	☐	☐	☐
Did not bring books or equipment required for the lesson	☐	☐	☐	☐
Worked well throughout the lesson	☐	☐	☐	☐
Wasted time in the lesson and was off task frequently	☐	☐	☐	☐
Completed all work in the lesson	☐	☐	☐	☐
Refused to do work in the lesson	☐	☐	☐	☐
Had to be moved away from other pupils in the lesson	☐	☐	☐	☐
Used unacceptable and abusive language in the lesson	☐	☐	☐	☐
Was aggressive in the lesson	☐	☐	☐	☐
Disrupted other pupils from getting on with their work	☐	☐	☐	☐
Got out of seat and wandered around the classroom	☐	☐	☐	☐
Left the classroom without permission	☐	☐	☐	☐
Refused to obey or follow the teacher's/TA's instructions	☐	☐	☐	☐
Ate in class without permission	☐	☐	☐	☐
Was rude to staff	☐	☐	☐	☐
Was rude to other pupils	☐	☐	☐	☐
Interfered with equipment and/or other pupils' work	☐	☐	☐	☐
Talked when the teacher was talking	☐	☐	☐	☐
Shouted out in class	☐	☐	☐	☐
Threw things around the classroom	☐	☐	☐	☐
Unable to work co-operatively with other pupils	☐	☐	☐	☐

Which three behaviours require targeting for improvement?   **Strategies to be used to make the improvements**

-

-

-

Figure 2.4 Tracking individual pupil behaviour over a day

From Rita Cheminais (2010), *Special Educational Needs for Newly Qualified Teachers and Teaching Assistants*, 2nd edn. London: Routledge. © 2010 Rita Cheminais

Table 2.12

Every Child Matters outcomes across the curriculum

	Be healthy	Stay safe	Enjoy and achieve	Make a positive contribution	Achieve economic well-being
What pupils need to learn	• importance of eating sensibly, staying physically active and getting enough rest • how to make positive choices and take sensible actions • how to protect their emotional, social and mental well-being • the long-term consequences of the lifestyle choices they make now	• how to identify and minimise risk • how to make informed, safe choices • how to voice their opinions and resist unhelpful peer pressure	• how to work imaginatively and creatively to develop new ideas, insights and ways of doing things • how to assess their skills, achievements and potential in order to set personal goals and achieve their best • the joy to be gained from successful learning	• to form positive relationships and avoid bullying and discriminatory behaviour • about the different roles that people play in a community • how they can contribute to their own school and the wider community • how to work effectively with others	• about the global economy and how businesses work • the qualities and skills needed for adult working life • to be enterprising • how to manage their own money
Art and Design	Exploring and expressing personal concerns and emotions	Following safe practices in the working environment; forming and expressing opinions about art; exploring identity and place in the world	Participating in creative, meaningful and intelligent making; expressing themselves in new and original ways; working in active learning environments	Collaborating with others on projects; exploring the role of art, craft and design across times and cultures	Developing skills in critical thinking and creative problem solving; learning about the creative industries; working with artists and designers
Citizenship	Being empowered through taking action and making decisions; learning about identity, diversity and respecting difference; learning about the politics of everyday life	Asking questions rather than taking things at face value; forming and expressing opinions; making responsible decisions; exploring controversial issues and situations; examining the consequences of different	Participating in decision making; working with others to campaign for change; taking part in debates and finding out more about local and global issues; using ICT or media such as film, drama and art to present and express ideas	Taking action on real issues and problems facing individuals and communities; working with others to try to influence change or resist unwanted change; developing the knowledge, skills and confidence to participate	Finding creative solutions to problems; expressing ideas and views effectively; negotiating; influencing others; learning about economic dimensions of political and social decisions; exploring the choices that governments have to make

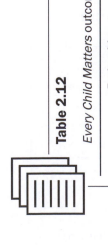

Subject					
		actions; learning how to seek help and advice; reducing risk when working in the wider community		effectively, responsibly and democratically; lobbying or campaigning on issues	regarding taxation and public spending priorities
Design and Technology	Understanding food hygiene; learning about the relationship between food, health, growth and energy balance; learning to prepare healthy food; investigating products to protect health	Following safe practices in the workshop; managing risk when using tools and equipment; thinking about the safety of others	Creating practical products in response to people's needs or wants; researching ideas and engaging with the world beyond school	Engaging in collaborative problem-solving activities; designing products that contribute positively to the community or environment	Generating practical cost-effective solutions that are relevant and fit for purpose; solving technical problems; responding creatively to briefs; developing proposals; working with designers; exploring career opportunities in design
English	Reading and writing for pleasure; exploring issues and expressing feelings through prose, poetry, drama and role play; reading to access health information	Developing the confidence to ask questions and express opinions; assessing the validity of opinions and information; exploring situations, dilemmas and relationships through texts, role play and drama	Experiencing the richness and breadth of literature; expressing ideas and opinions; creating new worlds in poetry and narrative; developing confidence through drama	Working collaboratively as part of a group discussion or drama activities; providing constructive responses to others' work; speaking, listening and writing for purposes beyond the classroom; contributing to school life through drama	Developing communication skills and literacy; expressing ideas and views effectively; exploring career opportunities in the creative and cultural industries
Geography	Investigating illness and disease around the world; comparing lifestyles in different countries	Developing safe working practices while carrying out fieldwork; exploring hazards and health risks in areas where people are not safe; questioning information and not taking things at face value	Learning about different environments, places, cultures and peoples; taking part in fieldwork; developing a sense of curiosity about the Earth	Considering their role as world citizens; learning about sustainable development; examining the social, environmental and economic impacts of what people do individually and collectively	Exploring how nations and peoples trade; researching, presenting and analysing information; appreciating the need for sustainable economic developments
History	Learning about personal and public health and their impact on life; exploring individual identity through personal and community history.	Developing safe working practices while carrying out fieldwork and other investigations; exploring events in the past when people have not been safe;	Discovering rich and varied stories from the past; taking part in investigations and fieldwork; visiting museums, galleries and historical sites; connecting	Learning about the lives of famous philanthropists; researching local history to find out who has helped to improve the community and how; learning how	Exploring how working patterns and the nature of work have changed over time; challenging information and being aware of bias and inaccuracies; expressing ideas

From Rita Cheminais (2010), *Special Educational Needs for Newly Qualified Teachers and Teaching Assistants*, 2nd edn. London: Routledge. © 2010 Rita Cheminais

Table 2.12 continued

Every Child Matters outcomes across the curriculum

	Be healthy	Stay safe	Enjoy and achieve	Make a positive contribution	Achieve economic well-being
		challenging information and being aware of bias and inaccuracies	life today to life in the past	populations have pulled together in times of war	and views effectively; engaging in critical research
ICT	Accessing information on health and well-being; analysing nutritional data; using monitoring technology during exercise	Developing safe practice when using ICT (e.g. correct positioning of equipment and chairs, taking regular breaks); questioning information and not accepting it at face value; learning responsible use of email and the internet; avoiding disclosure of personal details	Using ICT to support creativity, initiative and independent thinking; conveying ideas in original ways; using ICT to work collaboratively; using ICT for music, film and photography	Accessing information and ideas on local, national and international issues; sharing information with people from diverse backgrounds; learning about equality of access, copyright and plagiarism; using forums	Learning when and how to use ICT skills to support work; developing ICT capability; obtaining, analysing and presenting information; using ICT to collaborate with others; learning how to manage finances online
Mathematics	Investigating numerical data related to health and diet; becoming financially capable and gaining greater control over factors affecting health	Understanding risk through the study of probability; making informed choices about investments, loans and gambling	Developing mathematical ways of perceiving the world; recognising underlying structures and connections between mathematical ideas; investigating games and strategies	Learning to use logic, data and generalisations with precision	Understanding and managing money; making sound economic decisions in daily life; learning about investments; reasoning with numbers; interpreting graphs and diagrams; communicating maths information
Modern foreign language	Building confidence through speaking another language; gaining new perspective on the world and life in other countries	Communicating with strangers, dealing with unfamiliar situations in which communication is difficult; understanding others' customs and avoiding difficult or	Extending horizons beyond this country; learning to communicate with people from different parts of the world; learning about different cultures and countries; gaining a sense	Actively trying to understand and communicate with others; learning to be 'ambassadors' for their own country and culture	Learning to use business-related language; preparing to work in the international market

		dangerous situations in travel	of achievement from successful communication		
Music	Improving physical, mental and emotional-well being through singing, playing and listening to music	Developing critical skills and self-discipline; forming and expressing opinions about music	Gaining enjoyment from performing, composing and listening; taking part in musical activities and events; playing music with others	Contributing to school life as a performer, listener, organiser, music leader or in a supporting role	Working as part of a team to play or compose music; learning about the music industry
PE	Taking part in high-quality physical activity; developing a fitness programme; seeing physical activity as part of a life-long healthy lifestyle; expressing emotions through dance; enjoying watching sport; learning about how the body works and why exercise and rest are important; exploring dietary habits	Learning the importance of following rules; taking part safely in outdoor and adventurous activities; minimising risk in physical activity	Participating and achieving as performers, officials and leaders; making links with physical activities, sport and dance in the community; taking part in creative, artistic, aesthetic, competitive and challenging activities; working as part of a team	Contributing to school life through sport; helping as an official, coach or administrator; contributing to a team performance; developing an understanding of fairness; working collaboratively on problem-solving challenges	Working individually and as part of a team; reviewing, refining and carrying out plans; learning about balancing work with leisure and social interaction; exploring career opportunities in sport
PSHE	Learning about diet and healthy living; developing drug awareness; learning about sexual health; exploring self-identity and image; managing risk and dealing with social and moral dilemmas; withstanding peer pressure	Managing risk; developing safe working practices while engaged in work experience and enterprise activities; exploring personal, ethical and moral issues; developing first aid skills; forming safe relationships; avoiding debt and financial hardship	Learning practical, real-life skills; taking part in enterprise activities; meeting new people	Working collaboratively on group activities; getting involved with the local community	Learning about progression routes into further education, employment and training; finding creative solutions to problems; learning to be adaptable; expressing ideas and views effectively; working well in groups; engaging in critical research; evaluating evidence; identifying and analysing different interpretations of issues and events; substantiating arguments and judgements

From Rita Cheminais (2010), *Special Educational Needs for Newly Qualified Teachers and Teaching Assistants*, 2nd edn. London: Routledge. © 2010 Rita Cheminais

Table 2.12 continued

Every Child Matters outcomes across the curriculum

	Be healthy	Stay safe	Enjoy and achieve	Make a positive contribution	Achieve economic well-being
RE	Exploring morals and decision making; learning about sexual health and ethics; exploring mediation and enlightenment; learning about spiritual rituals	Evaluating ideas, relationships and practices; learning about religious and ethical rules governing care of children, respect for friends and neighbours and responsibility for crime; learning about authority, ethics, relationships and rights and responsibilities	Exploring and sharing beliefs, practices and feelings; engaging with issues of meaning and value; developing curiosity about religion in the modern world; searching for meaning; debating ideas; meeting people of different cultures and beliefs	Developing an appreciation of different points of view, investigating, discussing and building reasoned arguments; dealing with different beliefs respectfully; learning about justice, authority and interfaith dialogue; learning about faith groups in the community	Learning about religious and ethical rules surrounding the use of money; learning about equality, justice, prejudice, discrimination, human rights, fair trade, the environment and climate change; learning about religious issues in the workplace, such as diet, clothing, use of time for prayer, values and attitudes; learning about the work of charities; developing skills of listening, empathy and group collaboration
Science	Learning about diets, drugs, disease and contraception; understanding the consequences of poor diet and the misuse of alcohol and drugs	Following safe working practices in a laboratory; assessing and managing risk through scientific experiments; handling chemicals and biological materials safely; using electricity, heat and light safely	Developing curiosity about the world; carrying out practical investigations; exploring the effect of science on lives on a personal, local, national and global scale	Actively contributing to scientific investigations; learning about the relationship between science, society and the future of the world; considering ethical and moral issues; learning about global sustainability	Obtaining, analysing, evaluating and communicating data; engaging in critical research; exploring career opportunities in science

Source: adapted from *Every Child Matters at the heart of the curriculum*, QCA (2008).

From Rita Cheminais (2010), *Special Educational Needs for Newly Qualified Teachers and Teaching Assistants*, 2nd edn. London: Routledge. © 2010 Rita Cheminais

Ofsted in partnership with the DCSF produced a set of school-level indicators for evaluating pupils' well-being, which were introduced in September 2009 as part of the revised inspection framework. The indicators are quantitative and qualitative. It is important for trainee and newly qualified teachers and TAs to be aware of these, so that they can gather appropriate evidence on them from their everyday practice to feed into the school's Ofsted self-evaluation form.

In relation to the quantitative indicators, class teachers will need to monitor:

- the annual attendance rate for pupils in the class;
- the percentage of pupils in the class who are persistent absentees, i.e. miss 20 per cent or more of schooling;
- the percentage of pupils in the class undertaking at least two hours a week of PE and sport;
- the take-up of school lunches by pupils in the class;
- the rate of any permanent exclusions from the class;
- the percentage of pupils who participate in learning on leaving school (for the secondary phase).

In relation to the qualitative indicators, based on the perceptions of pupils and their parents/carers from surveys about the school's contribution to promoting pupil well-being, class teachers will need to consider how they:

- ensure pupils feel safe in school and in the classroom;
- know if any pupils experience being bullied by peers;
- ensure pupils know which adult to approach in school if they have any concerns;
- know if pupils in the class enjoy school and their learning;
- know if pupils in the class are making good progress;
- know if pupils in the class feel they are listened to;
- give pupils opportunities to influence decisions in the school;
- promote healthy eating;
- promote exercise and a healthy lifestyle, and, for younger children, play;
- discourage smoking, consumption of alcohol and the use of illegal drugs and other harmful substances;
- give good guidance on relationships and sexual health;
- help pupils to manage their feelings and develop resilience;
- promote equality and counteract discrimination;
- provide a good range of educational, including extra-curricular, activities;
- give pupils good opportunities to contribute to the local community;
- help pupils from different backgrounds to get on well together;
- help pupils to gain the knowledge and skills they will need in the future;
- offer pupils the opportunity at the age of 14 to access a range of curriculum choices;
- help pupils to make choices that will help them progress towards a chosen career or a subject for further study.

Table 2.13 offers a quick guide to busy trainee and newly qualified teachers and teaching assistants on the evidence Ofsted inspectors will seek in relation to the *ECM* well-being outcomes, as part of everyday classroom practice.

Table 2.13

Every Child Matters outcomes for children and young people

ECM outcomes	ECM aims	Ofsted evidence
Be healthy	Physically healthy Mentally and emotionally healthy Sexually healthy Healthy lifestyles Choose not to take illegal drugs Parents, carers and families promote healthy choices	Pupils take regular exercise, including two hours' PE/sport per week, and they know how to maintain good physical health Pupils show a good understanding of how they can live a healthy lifestyle, and they can make informed healthy lifestyle choices Pupils understand sexual health risks, the dangers of smoking and substance abuse Pupils eat and drink healthily in school Pupils can recognise the signs of personal stress and they know how to manage it Pupils can access appropriate support if they feel troubled and worried Pupils are consulted on and are involved in any decision making related to their health
Stay safe	Safe from maltreatment, neglect, violence and sexual exploitation Safe from accidental injury and death Safe from bullying and discrimination Safe from crime and anti-social behaviour in and out of school Have security, stability and are cared for Parents, carers and families provide safe home and stability	Pupils display concern for others and refrain from intimidating and anti-social behaviour Pupils feel safe from bullying, discrimination and racism Pupils feel confident to report bullying and any racist incidents Pupils have regard to the dignity, safety and well-being of others Pupils respect the wishes of others Pupils do not behave anti-socially Pupils know their views are listened to and are confident with the adult support provided Pupils act responsibly and are able to assess risk Pupils are protected from danger in school Physical activities are undertaken in an orderly and sensible manner Pupils are receptive to the support and help given to them by other agencies
Enjoy and achieve	Ready for school Attend and enjoy school Achieve stretching national educational standards at primary school Achieve personal and social development and enjoy recreation Achieve stretching national educational standards at secondary school Parents, carers and families support learning	Pupils have positive attitudes to learning and education Pupils behave well and have a good school attendance record Pupils make good progress in relation to their starting points Pupils achieve their optimum potential Pupils enjoy their learning very much and their achievements are valued Pupils' learning needs are catered for through personalised curriculum pathways Pupils participate in recreational lunchtime and after-school activities Pupils are active participants in their own learning and in aspects of school life

Table 2.13 continued

Every Child Matters outcomes for children and young people

ECM outcomes	ECM aims	Ofsted evidence
		Good personal development evidenced by high self-esteem
		High aspirations and increasing independence
Make a positive contribution	Engage in decision making and support the community and environment	Pupils are able to form stable relationships with others
	Engage in law-abiding and positive behaviour in and out of school	Pupils are able to manage change in their own lives
	Develop positive relationships and choose not to bully and discriminate	Pupils show social responsibility and refrain from bullying and discrimination
	Develop self-confidence and successfully deal with significant life changes and challenges	Pupils are able to express their views at school, they are confident that their views and 'voice' will be heard, and they participate in decision making on school matters
	Develop enterprising behaviour	Pupils show a good commitment to supporting others in school and in the community
	Parents, carers and families promote positive behaviour	Pupils engage with volunteering activities
		Pupils subscribe to the school's view about what makes a worthwhile positive contribution
		Pupils understand their legal and civil rights and responsibilities and how to become a responsible citizen
		Pupils make positive progress following transfer and transition between key stages and phases of education
Achieve economic well-being	Engage in further education, employment or training on leaving school	Pupils develop basic skills in literacy, numeracy and ICT
	Ready for employment	Pupils develop their self-confidence
	Live in decent homes and sustainable communities	Pupils are able to work independently and co-operatively with others
	Access to transport and material goods	Pupils can take initiative and calculate risk when making decisions
	Live in households free from low income	Pupils have developed financial literacy and gain an understanding of business and the economy, and of their career options
	Parents, carers and families are supported to be economically active	Pupils have a knowledge of enterprise and they participate in enterprising activities such as fundraising for charity
		Pupils have the skills to prepare them for later life – work and adulthood

Useful resources relating to meeting the needs of SEN/LDD pupils

Web-based resources

Special Educational Needs is a series of Teachers TV videos that focus on meeting a range of SEN in primary and secondary mainstream classrooms. The programmes cover the following aspects of SEN: dyslexia, autistic spectrum disorder, visual/hearing impairment. It also has a feature on special schools. There are also links to further resources and useful organisations. Further information about how to view or download these videos is at http://www.teachers.tv/node%252F23458

The TTRB website has a resource bank of materials that offer scenarios with practical strategies on how to manage pupil behaviour in the mainstream classroom. You can view the powerpoint presentations and download information from the website http://www.behaviour4learning.ac.uk/

The TTRB video *Make Them Go Away – An Anti-Bullying Video on SEN* is a five-minute drama presentation set in a secondary school to show how to help pupils deal with their feelings. It can be downloaded from http://www.ttrb.ac.uk/Browse2.aspx?anchorId=17790&selectId=17816

Teachers TV video *Teaching with Bayley – Love 'Em or Loathe 'Em* shows how to manage pupil behaviour in the secondary classroom. It can be viewed at http://www.teachers.tv/node%25F5463

The government's Inclusion Development Programme (IDP) interactive web-based resources can be accessed at the website http://www.standards.dfes.gov.uk/primary/features/inclusion/sen/idp

The resources help to identify approaches and strategies for removing barriers to learning for each of the types of learning difficulties or disabilities covered. Onscreen presentations provide helpful information which can be transferred to early years, primary and secondary mainstream settings. They are aimed at trainee and newly qualified teachers and those wishing to update their knowledge and skills in working with SEN pupils. Teaching assistants will also find the IDP a useful resource. The programme will be added to during 2009 and 2010. The current resources available focus on dyslexia, speech, language and communication needs, and autistic spectrum disorders.

Useful publications

Association of Teachers and Lecturers (1997) *Managing Classroom Behaviour*, London: Association of Teaching and Lecturers

Association of Teachers and Lecturers (2002) *Achievement for All. Working with Children with Special Educational Needs in Mainstream Schools and Colleges*, London: Association of Teaching and Lecturers

Briggs, Sue (2004) *Inclusion and How to Do It. Meeting SEN in Secondary Classrooms*, Abingdon: David Fulton/Routledge

Briggs, Sue (2005) *Inclusion and How to Do It. Meeting SEN in Primary Classrooms*, Abingdon: David Fulton/Routledge

Cheminais, Rita (2004) *How to Create the Inclusive Classroom. Removing Barriers to Learning*, with CD, Abingdon: David Fulton/Routledge

Cheminais, Rita (2008) *Every Child Matters. A Practical Guide for Teaching Assistants*, Abingdon: Routledge

Cheminais, Rita (2009) *The Pocket Guide to Every Child Matters*, Abingdon: Routledge

DfES (2000) *Teaching Assistant File: Induction Training for Teaching Assistants in Primary Schools*, London: Department for Education and Skills

DfES (2000) *Teaching Assistant File: Induction Training for Teaching Assistants in Secondary Schools*, London: Department for Education and Skills

East, Viv and Evans, Linda (2006) *At a Glance. A Practical Guide to Children's Special Needs*, London: Continuum

Fox, Glenys (2001) *Supporting Children with Behaviour Difficulties. A Guide for Assistants in Schools*, London: David Fulton/Routledge

Halliwell, Marian (2003) *Supporting Children with Special Educational Needs. A Guide for Assistants in Schools and Pre-Schools*, London: David Fulton/Routledge

Kirby, Amanda (2005) *Mapping SEN: Routes through Identification and Intervention*, with CD, Abingdon: David Fulton/Routledge

Overall, Lyn (2007) *Supporting Children's Learning. A Guide for Teaching Assistants*, London: Sage

The series *Meeting SEN in the Curriculum* (2004) London: David Fulton/Routledge, comprises thirteen books aimed at the secondary phase of education. They all have an accompanying CD which contains useful resources.

The series by Hull Learning Services (2004) *Supporting Children*, London: David Fulton/Routledge, comprises eleven books covering a range of different special educational needs, which offer practical tips and strategies for including children with SEN/LDD in the mainstream primary school.

Questions for reflection

- How have you developed and promoted positive behaviour for learning among the SEN/LDD pupils you teach and support?

- Which aspects of behaviour management do you need to develop further and how will you address this?

- How can you make better use of ICT in your teaching or support work with SEN/LDD pupils?

- Which aspect of quality-first teaching poses the greatest challenge for you, and how will you further develop your practice in this aspect?

- How are you ensuring that the learning resources you use in lessons take account of diversity to promote inclusion?

- To what extent are you developing emotional literacy in the classroom?

- Which aspects of personalised learning have worked well and which have not worked as well? How will you improve those aspects that haven't worked as well?

- Which aspects of SEN knowledge do you consider you need to develop further, and how will you address this?

- How far do you agree or disagree with the statement: 'Personalised learning is inclusion on the cheap.'?

- How far do you agree or disagree that quality-first teaching can successfully meet the needs of all pupils with SEN/LDD in the mainstream classroom?

CHAPTER 3

Assessing SEN/LDD pupil progress, monitoring and evaluating personalised provision

This chapter will cover:

- Professional and occupational standards for teachers and TAs relating to assessment, monitoring and evaluating personalised provision for pupils with SEN/LDD
- Assessment for learning for pupils with SEN/LDD
- Tracking the progress of pupils with SEN/LDD
- Expectations for the progress of pupils with SEN/LDD
- RAISEonline and SEN pupil level attainment data
- Monitoring and evaluating personalised provision for pupils with SEN/LDD
- Meeting the Ofsted inspection requirements
- Useful resources relating to assessment, monitoring and evaluation
- Further activities

Professional and occupational standards for teachers and TAs relating to assessment, monitoring and evaluating personalised provision for pupils with SEN/LDD

Table 3.1 outlines the QTS, NQT induction and national occupational standards relevant to teaching assistants in relation to managing, monitoring and evaluating additional provision or interventions for SEN/LDD pupils.

Assessment for learning for pupils with SEN/LDD

According to the Assessment Reform Group (2002), assessment for learning is the process of seeking and interpreting evidence for use by pupils and their teachers to decide where the pupils are in their learning, where they need to go next, and how best to get there.

Utilising assessment for learning helps to guide classroom practice for all pupils, including those with SEN/LDD, because it:

- informs planning for teaching and learning and enables teaching and learning support to be adjusted by taking account of assessment results;

Table 3.1

National standards for teachers and TAs on assessing pupil progress, monitoring and evaluating personalised provision

QTS standards	Induction standards for NQTs	National occupational standards for TAs
Professional knowledge and understanding **Assessment and monitoring** Q11 Know the assessment requirements and arrangements for the subjects/curriculum areas they are trained to teach, including those relating to public examinations and qualifications Q12 Know a range of approaches to assessment, including the importance of formative assessment Q13 Know how to use local and national statistical information to evaluate the effectiveness of their teaching, to monitor the progress of those they teach and to raise levels of attainment **Professional skills** **Planning** Q22 Plan for progression across the age and ability range for which they are trained, designing effective learning sequences within lessons and across series of lessons and demonstrating secure subject/curriculum knowledge **Assessing, monitoring and giving feedback** Q26 (a) Make effective use of a range of assessment, monitoring and recording strategies Q26 (b) Assess the learning needs of those they teach in order to set challenging learning objectives Q27 Provide timely, accurate and constructive feedback on learners' attainment, progress and areas for development	**3 Professional knowledge and understanding** **i. Pedagogic practice** C11 Know the assessment requirements and arrangements for the subjects/curriculum areas they teach, including those relating to public examinations and qualifications C12 Know a range of approaches to assessment including the importance of formative assessment C13 Know how to use local and national statistical information to evaluate the effectiveness of their teaching to monitor the progress of those they teach and to raise levels of attainment C14 Know how to use reports and other sources of external information related to assessment in order to provide learners with accurate and constructive feedback on their strengths, weaknesses, attainment, progress and areas for development, including action plans for improvement **4 Professional skills** **i. Planning and assessment** C26 Plan for progression across the age and ability range they teach, designing effective learning sequences within lessons and across series of lessons informed by secure subject/curriculum knowledge C31 Make effective use of an appropriate range of observation, assessment, monitoring and recording strategies as a basis for setting challenging learning objectives and monitoring learners' progress and levels of attainment	**NVQ Level 2** STL9 Observe and report on pupil performance in order to gather evidence of their knowledge, understanding and skills **NVQ Level 3** STL23 Plan, deliver and evaluate teaching and learning activities under the direction of a teacher STL24 Contribute to the planning and evaluation of teaching and learning activities STL29 Observe and promote pupil performance and development in order to gather evidence of their knowledge, understanding and skills and to plan with the teacher to improve pupil support STL30 Contribute to assessment for learning in order to promote pupils' learning and to enable them to review their own learning STL51 Contribute to improving attendance by monitoring pupils' attendance STL55 Contribute to maintaining pupil records by collecting and inputting pupil data

Table 3.1 continued

National standards for teachers and TAs on assessing pupil progress, monitoring and evaluating personalised provision

QTS standards	Induction standards for NQTs	National occupational standards for TAs
Q28 Support and guide learners to reflect on their learning, identify the progress they have made and identify their emerging learning needs	C33 Support and guide learners so that they can reflect on their learning, identify the progress they have made, set positive targets for improvement and become successful independent learners	
Reviewing teaching and learning	C36 Review the impact of the feedback provided to learners and guide learners on how to improve their attainment	
Q29 Evaluate the impact of their teaching on the progress of all learners, and modify their planning and classroom practice where necessary	**ii. Teaching**	
	C34 Use assessment as part of their teaching to diagnose learners' needs, set realistic and challenging targets for improvement, and plan future teaching	
	5 Developing practice **Standards**	
	C35 Review the effectiveness of their teaching and its impact on learners' progress, attainment and well-being, refining their approaches where necessary	

Source: TDA (2007a, 2007b, 2007c).

- focuses on knowing how pupils learn;
- actively involves pupils in their own learning;
- builds pupils' self-esteem and enhances their motivation to learn;
- supports pupils' self-assessment and peer-assessment, helping them to know how to improve;
- provides a vehicle for giving pupils feedback on their learning and work;
- enables pupils to take greater responsibility and ownership for their own progress.

Effective daily assessment for learning strategies includes:

- using prompting and probing questions to assess pupils' understanding, giving SEN/LDD pupils extra thinking time to respond to questions;
- making planned observations of SEN/LDD pupils during teaching and learning so as to help identify barriers to learning and participation;
- holding focused discussions with SEN/LDD pupils about their work and learning, to enable them to reflect upon their progress and to articulate successes against targets set;

- analysing SEN/LDD pupils' work and giving them constructive feedback to guide further improvement;

- engaging SEN/LDD pupils in the assessment for learning process through the use of paired peer assessment to discuss and reflect on the learning strategies used.

Useful pupil self-assessment and peer-assessment approaches

The following assessment approaches help SEN/LDD pupils to assess their own work and that of another peer.

- Use of traffic light colours to highlight their work: red means pupils have not achieved the task and feel confused; amber means they feel they have made some progress, but are uncertain about certain things/aspects; green means they have achieved and feel confident.

- Use of thumbs as a sign of achievement and understanding: thumbs down means they are struggling with the work, are unclear about what to do and would welcome help; thumbs sideways means they are not sure but think they are OK, but their work might need checking; and thumbs up means great, they understand the work and feel they are doing well.

- Use by teacher/TA of prompt questions which are displayed on the classroom wall: *What areas of your work do you think could be improved and how/why? What did you find the hardest to do and where can you get further help? What are we learning (WALT), What I'm looking for (WILF) in the work/lesson is . . .? This is because (TIB) . . . The three things I have learnt in today's lesson are . . .*

- Examples of what a particular National Curriculum or P scale level looks like in anonymous pieces of work, matched to the relevant assessment criteria.

When giving SEN/LDD pupils constructive oral feedback on their work it is important to use positive language when they find a task difficult, e.g. 'It's making you think because you are learning something new.'

Assessment for learning enables trainee and newly qualified teachers and TAs to identify:

- what helps or hinders the SEN/LDD pupils' access to the curriculum and learning;

- the impact of their teaching and support on SEN/LDD pupils' learning;

- the strengths and the talents SEN/LDD pupils have;

- the gaps, misconceptions and misunderstandings SEN/LDD pupils may have in their learning;

- appropriate and relevant learning targets;

- the pupils' views of their own learning strengths and weaknesses.

Table 3.2 offers some useful strategies to support assessment for learning.

Assessing pupils' well-being

Assessing pupils' well-being against the five *Every Child Matters* (*ECM*) outcomes is an ongoing process as part of everyday practice. Trainee and newly qualified teachers and TAs will be able to use the assessment evidence from observations, pupil-level well-being data, and pupils' views and perceptions to help identify:

- whether SEN/LDD pupils are making good enough progress in relation to their well-being;

- whether SEN/LDD pupils are 'stuck', or are not making good enough progress in any of the *ECM* well-being outcomes or aspects thereof;

- which *ECM* outcomes SEN/LDD pupils make the most progress in;

- which *ECM* outcomes SEN/LDD pupils make the least progress in and why;

- what action needs to be taken in order to address any gaps or lack of progress in SEN/LDD pupils' well-being.

Table 3.3 illustrates the criteria for judging pupils' *ECM* well-being.

Table 3.2

Useful strategies for supporting assessment for learning

Key characteristics of assessment for learning	Strategies to use with pupils, including those with SEN/LDD
Sharing the learning objectives with the pupils	• Share learning objectives at the beginning of lessons and at various points throughout, in language that the pupils understand • Use the objectives as the basis for targeted questioning during the lesson and in plenaries • Relate the learning to the 'big picture' of the topic
Helping pupils to know and recognise the standards for which they are aiming	• Show pupils work that has met assessment criteria and explain why • Model what the work should look and sound like • Explain what you are looking for, using clear success criteria, and relate this to the learning objectives • Ensure that there are clear expectations about the pupils' presentation of work • Provide displays that show 'work in progress' as well as finished pieces • Have prompts for success criteria on posters or in the backs of books, e.g. 'to get to Level 5 I need to . . .'
Involving pupils in peer- and self-assessment	• Give pupils opportunities to talk about what they have learned and what they have found difficult with reference to the learning objectives • Encourage pupils to discuss their work together, focusing on how to improve • Ask pupils to explain their thinking and reasoning • Give time for pupils to reflect on their learning together
Providing feedback that leads pupils to recognise their next steps and how to take them	• Give value via positive and specific oral feedback • In marking, relate to the assessment success criteria: identify what the pupil has done well, what needs to be done to improve it and how this should be done • Identify next steps in learning
Promoting confidence that every pupil can improve	• To boost confidence, identify the small steps so that pupils can see their progress for themselves • Develop an ethos of support and encouragement among the class
Involving both the teacher and pupil in reviewing and reflecting on assessment information	• Reflect with pupils on their work and the learning processes involved • Reward efforts to contribute and think about what learning has been gained in the lesson

Source: DfES (2005c: 15).

Table 3.3 Criteria for assessing pupil well-being

Be healthy	Stay safe	Enjoy and achieve	Make a positive contribution	Achieve economic well-being
• Pupils eat healthy meals at lunchtime	• Pupils consider the safety of others	• Pupils' achievements are valued	• Pupils' views and opinions are listened to	• Pupils have opportunities to participate in mini-enterprise activities
• Pupils drink water throughout the day	• Pupils report bullying incidents to a member of staff	• Pupils' attendance and punctuality is good	• Pupils complete an annual survey	• Pupils engage in problem solving
• Pupils undertake at least two hours of PE/sport each week	• Pupils follow safety rules and warning signs about hazards and dangers	• Pupils are engaged in setting targets	• Pupils can post their ideas in a suggestion box	• Pupils communicate effectively with others
• Pupils keep the learning environment clean, tidy and litter free	• Pupils play safely at all times	• Pupils regularly review their own progress and discuss it with staff	• Pupils follow a Pupils' Charter	• Pupils are financially literate and can manage their own money/savings
• Pupils participate in outdoor play	• Pupils work safely in lessons	• Pupils' work and achievements are displayed	• Pupils are able to raise issues with the school council	• Pupils know about the businesses in the local area
• Pupils know which trusted adult/key worker to go to in school when worried	• Pupils are aware of safety in the community, e.g. stranger danger, road safety	• Pupils participate in practical work and co-operative learning	• Pupils participate in fund raising and volunteering	• Pupils can access study support
• Pupils have a quiet area or place to go to in school when they need it	• Pupils follow safety rules on school trips	• Pupils use different learning styles	• Pupils vote on important school issues	• Pupils can take positions of responsibility
• Pupils respect the feelings and views of others	• Pupils use equipment correctly under adult supervision	• Pupils use ICT to support learning	• Pupils know their rights (UNCRC)	• Pupils know how to cope with change
• Pupils have access to further information about healthy eating and healthy lifestyles	• Chemicals and medicines are stored safely and securely	• Pupils participate in extended school activities	• Pupils can access peer mentoring and buddy systems	• Pupil initiative is encouraged
• Pupils know how to manage their feelings and emotions and build resilience	• Access routes are kept clear for wheelchair users	• Pupils work with artists in residence, sports coaches, external experts	• Pupils participate in law-abiding behaviour	• Pupils have been given advice on future learning and career pathways
	• Outdoor areas are well lit and secure	• Pupil behaviour is good	• Pupils do not bully or discriminate against others and act as advocates for others	• Pupils have developed basic ICT numeracy, literacy skills

Assessing the behaviour of pupils

The QCA, in partnership with the DfEE, published in 2001 sets of emotional and behavioural development scales to enable teachers and those who support pupils aged 5 to 16 to measure their progress in the aspects of emotional and behavioural development.

The emotional and behavioural development scales comprise performance indicators for conduct behaviour, emotional behaviour and learning behaviour. Each category of behaviour has five indicators, which are rated on a scale of 0 (not at all) to 5 (always). Pupils could score a maximum of 75 if they achieved 5 for each of the fifteen indicators.

Using the scale for emotional and behavioural development helps to identify aspects of pupils' behaviour that require targeting for further improvement. Assessment using the scale should be carried out at the end of a term or over a three-month period in one sitting. Assessments can be made for an individual, a group of pupils in a class or an entire class in a particular year group. It is important that the scores are moderated between staff to ensure consistency in the judgements being made.

You can download the emotional and behavioural development scales from the QCA website at: http://www.qca.org.uk/qca_8401.aspx

Tracking the progress of pupils with SEN/LDD

Tracking the progress of pupils is essential to promote the achievement of high standards. Ongoing assessment forms the basis of the tracking. Pupils' progress in learning, behaviour, attendance and *ECM* well-being is usually formally tracked and monitored each term or half yearly, using a range of performance information such as teacher assessment, test results, outcomes from staff pupil progress meetings, and discussions with pupils. Tracking information is used formatively to inform any modifications necessary in relation to teaching and learning, behaviour management and *ECM* well-being.

Tracking pupil progress is a well-established practice in schools, which helps trainee, newly qualified and experienced teachers and TAs to:

- check pupil progress towards meeting individual targets set;

- track ongoing progress, particularly when additional interventions have been put in place;

- provide a cross-check between teachers, teaching assistants and learning mentors on the progress pupils have made;

- monitor the progress of specific groups or cohorts of pupils, e.g. SEN/LDD or vulnerable pupils, to help identify and address any underachievement;

- identify particular strengths or areas of weakness among individual pupils or small groups of pupils in a subject or an aspect of a subject;

- inform any necessary revision of teaching and intervention programmes;

- demonstrate the value added progress obtained through the additional provision put in place for pupils with SEN/LDD;

- help raise teacher expectations in relation to actual and potential pupil performance;

- enable comparisons in pupil progress to be made periodically within and between schools in a local authority, as well as against national benchmarks.

The national primary and secondary strategies provide exemplars of grids that can be used to track pupil progress, particularly in English and Maths. Schools may also have their own pupil progress tracking sheets. Figure 3.1 gives an example of a generic tracking sheet which focuses on learning, behaviour and *ECM* well-being.

Expectations for the progress of pupils with SEN/LDD

According to the DCSF the majority of pupils with SEN/LDD in mainstream schools are working at National Curriculum levels. Ofsted in 2006 found that: 'Progress for different pupils with LDD could range from that which arrests or closes the attainment gap between the pupil and his or her peers, or which demonstrates an improvement in self-help, social or personal skills' (Ofsted 2006a: 15; paragraph 48).

Ofsted went on to determine what good progress for pupils with LDD was considered to be: 'This was usually a gain of two National Curriculum levels or two P levels (within the P scales), dependent on a pupil's starting point across a key stage' (Ofsted 2006a: 15; paragraph 51).

This finding by Ofsted resulted in the government's national expectation that pupils identified as having SEN/LDD will make at least two levels of progress at each key stage, with the exception of a small minority of pupils with significant learning difficulties or disabilities.

The *SEN Code of Practice* (DfES 2001c) defined adequate progress for pupils with SEN as being that which:

- closes the attainment gap between the pupil and their peers
- prevents the attainment gap growing wider
- is similar to that of peers starting from the same attainment baseline, but less than that of the majority of their peers
- matches or betters the pupil's previous rate of progress
- ensures access to the full curriculum
- demonstrates an improvement in self-help, social or personal skills
- demonstrates improvements in the pupil's behaviour
- is likely to lead to appropriate accreditation
- is likely to lead to participation in further education, training and/or employment.

(DfES 2001c: 52, 68; paragraphs 5.42, 6.49)

Progress among pupils with learning difficulties is also evident when they:

- develop their communication skills;
- develop their social interactions and participation with others and gain in confidence;
- can respond appropriately to events, experiences and the actions of others;
- are able to demonstrate the same achievement on more than one occasion and under changing circumstances;
- increase their knowledge and understanding of a subject;

	English			Mathematics				Science				ICT				DT	History	Geography	Art and Design	Music	PE	Modern foreign language	RE	PSHE
	1	2	3	1	2	3	4	1	2	3	4	1	2	3	4									
P level																								
NC level																								
EBD Conduct (25)																								
EBD Emotional (25)																								
EBD Learning (25)																								
ECM Healthy (0–4)																								
ECM Safe (0–4)																								
ECM Enjoy and achieve (0–4)																								
ECM positive contribution (0–4)																								
ECM Economic well-being (0–4)																								

Name of pupil: _____ Form/Class: _____ Date: _____

Figure 3.1 Tracking pupil progress in learning, behaviour and *ECM* well-being

From Rita Cheminais (2010), *Special Educational Needs for Newly Qualified Teachers and Teaching Assistants*, 2nd edn. London: Routledge. © 2010 Rita Cheminais

- require less adult or technological support to undertake a task;
- require less curriculum differentiation;
- can behave appropriately and cope with failure and frustration in learning.

The DCSF is in the process of producing guidance and training materials for teachers, which will help to clarify what making good progress looks like in English, Mathematics and Science for pupils with SEN/LDD. Ofsted HMI suggested a benchmark for expected rates of good progress for pupils with SEN/LDD, which is illustrated in Table 3.4.

The DCSF identifies three key principles of good progress for pupils with SEN/ LDD. They are as follows:

- having high expectations;
- using age and prior attainment to inform expectations;
- using moderation to improve the reliability of teacher assessment.

Table 3.4

Good and outstanding progress for learners with SEN/LDD

Year group	P level/ NC level	Good	Outstanding
Year 5			
Who at the end of Year 2 achieved	P1–P3	One level gain	One or more level gain
	P4–P7	More than one level	More than two level gains
	P8	Level gain to lower levels of NC Level 2	Gain to NC Level 2 or more
	NC Level 1	Level gain to lower levels of NC Level 3	Gain to NC Level 3 or more
	NC Level 2	Level gain to lower levels of NC Level 4	Gain to NC Level 4 or more
	NC Level 3	Level gain to lower levels of NC Level 5	Two level gains or more
	NC Level 4	Level gain to lower levels of NC Level 6	Lower NC Level 6 or more
Year 8			
Who at the end of Year 6 achieved	P1–P3	One sub-level gain	One or more level gain
	P4–P7	One level gain	More than one level
	P8	Level gain to NC Level 1	More than one level gain
	NC Level 1	Level gain to NC Level 2	More than one level gain
	NC Level 2	Level gain to NC Level 3	More than one level gain
	NC Level 3	Level gain to NC Level 4	More than one level gain
	NC Level 4	More than one level gain	More than two level gains
	NC Level 5	Two level gains	More than three level gains
	NC Level 6	More than two level gains	More than two-plus level gains
Year 10			
Who at the end of Year 6 achieved	P1–P3	One sub-level gain	One or more level gain
	P4–P7	One level gain	More than one level
	P8	Level gain to NC Level 1	More than one level gain
	NC Level 1	Level gain to NC Level 2	More than one level gain
	NC Level 2	Level gain to NC Level 3	More than one level gain
	NC Level 3	Level gain to lower levels of NC Level 5	Level gain to NC Level 5 or more
	NC Level 4	Level gain to lower levels of NC Level 6	Level gain to NC Level 6 or more
	NC Level 5	Level gain to lower levels of NC Level 7	Level gain to lower levels of NC Level 7 or more
	NC Level 6	More than one level gain	More than two level gains

Assessing pupil progress

Assessing pupil progress (APP), a DCSF initiative, complements the assessment for learning strategy. APP adopts a systematic, focused and structured approach to the periodic assessment of pupils' progress at Key Stages 1, 2 and 3 in Reading, Writing and Mathematics, and at Key Stage 3 in Science and ICT. The purpose of APP is to indicate the next learning steps for individual pupils (curricular targets), and identify areas of learning that need to be strengthened. SEN/LDD pupils benefit from teachers using the APP approach. A range of APP resources is available: the handbook, the standards file which exemplifies the national standards, assessment guidelines and a guidance booklet.

The APP process comprises seven steps. These are as follows:

1 Over a period of time, the outcomes to be assessed are decided upon and evidence is gathered which shows the pupils' attainment from daily teaching and learning.

2 An appropriate range of evidence, e.g. pupils' work and outcomes of discussions between pupils, and between teacher and pupils, is reviewed

3 The appropriate assessment guidelines sheet to build up a profile of a pupil's learning over time is chosen.

4 Teachers highlight the assessment criteria for which there is evidence available.

5 The pupil's developing profile of learning is used to decide whether attainment is low, secure or high, whether there is insufficient evidence, or whether the pupil is operating below level.

6 Teachers moderate assessments against criteria collectively to ensure reliability and consistency in judgements.

7 Adjustments to planning, teaching and intervention are made where necessary, if pupils are underperforming/underachieving.

Further information about APP can be found at www.qca.org.uk/assessment and on the national primary and secondary strategies website http://nationalstrategies. standards.dcsf.gov.uk/

Using the P scales

The P scales are differentiated performance criteria for assessing the attainment of SEN pupils aged 5 to 16 who are working below National Curriculum Level 1. There are P scales for each subject in the National Curriculum and also for RE and PSHE. The P scales comprise eight performance levels: P1 to P3 relate to early levels of general attainment, and P4 to P8 relate to subject attainment.

The national strategies website provides information and guidance to support the effective use of P scales, as well as case studies. The P scales support summative assessment at the end of a year or key stage. They help to track linear and lateral pupil progress, and inform target setting. They provide a best-fit judgement on SEN pupil performance. A pupil does not have to demonstrate every element of a P level descriptor to be given a P level.

It became mandatory from September 2007 for schools to provide P scale data for SEN pupils working below National Curriculum Level 1. The QCA produces a useful DVD with accompanying booklet on how to moderate the P scales in English, Mathematics and Science at levels P4 to P8.

Further information on the P scales, and the QCA DVD pack *Using the P Scales*, can be obtained from the websites http://www.qca.org.uk/qca_6624.aspx and http://www.qca.org.uk/qca_8541.aspx http://nationalstrategies.standards.dcsf.gov.uk/

RAISEonline and SEN pupil level attainment data

Reporting and Analysis for Improvement through School Self-Evaluation (RAISEonline) offers an interactive analysis of school and pupil performance data which aims to:

- enable schools to analyse and evaluate performance data in greater depth, e.g. at whole school, key stage, subject, pupil group, individual pupil and test question level;

- enable schools to create particular school-defined fields and teaching groups;

- inform and support improvement in the quality of teaching and learning;

- provide information to support whole-school target setting;

- provide a common dataset for use by the school, the LA, Ofsted and the school improvement partner.

RAISEonline as a web-based data system is password-protected to provide secure access to all pupil level data. If you are new to using RAISEonline it is useful first to book yourself an individual session with the assessment co-ordinator to look at the school's overall performance compared to national performance. Once you are familiar and feel confident with interpreting RAISEonline in the whole-school context, you can ask the assessment co-ordinator to provide you with SEN pupil level attainment data for those in your class group, which you can then analyse together with the TA, to help to inform future planning and provision.

Data in RAISEonline are illustrated in a range of ways. Beginners to data may find it easier to interpret the progress charts with stick pupils or with the scatter plots which illustrate the progress of SEN pupils as a distinct group, or in relation to their mainstream peers, across a key stage (referred to as the contextual value added progress), taking into account factors such as prior attainment, gender, free school meals, date of birth and ethnicity, compared with similar pupils in similar schools nationally.

Practical activity

Look at the scatter plot in Figure 3.2, which illustrates the contextual valued added analysis of SEN pupils' predicted (expected) outcome compared to their actual outcome in English, from KS1 to KS2, in a mainstream primary school located in an area of social deprivation.

Answer the following questions:

- Do you consider the SEN pupils at Action and Action Plus to be making sufficient progress across a key stage in this school?

- What questions might you wish to ask in relation to teacher assessment?

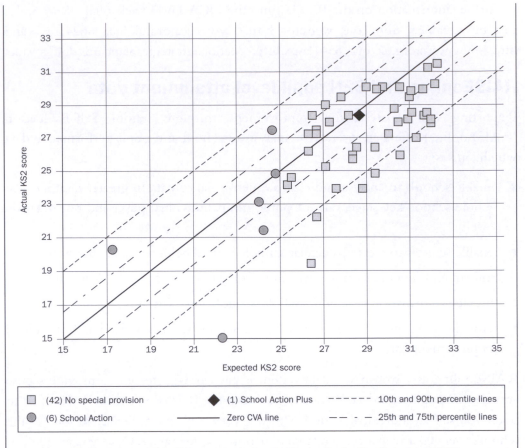

Figure 3.2 KS1 to KS2 CVA analysis by SEN pupils in English for 2009

- Given that some SEN pupils' needs may be more complex, particularly at Action Plus, what issues, if any, is the scatter plot raising about the effectiveness of SEN pupils' provision and interventions?

- What further RAISEonline filters might you wish to utilise in relation to further analysing the progress of SEN pupils in this school?

- Where a SEN pupil appears to be underachieving from the scatter plot data, what action would you take to address the issue?

Monitoring and evaluating personalised provision for pupils with SEN/LDD

All trainee and newly qualified teachers and TAs/LSAs need to monitor and evaluate the impact of their teaching and support on pupils' learning, as well as the impact of additional interventions on improving pupils' attainment, achievements and well-being outcomes. It is helpful to clarify what is meant by the terms monitoring and evaluation.

Monitoring refers to the ongoing checks on pupil progress over time, or on how a new policy or strategy is being implemented. Monitoring the impact of teaching, support for learning and additional provision to improve pupils' *ECM* well-being outcomes may include gathering evidence from the following sources:

- focused discussions between class/subject teachers and TAs/LSAs on pupil progress each term or half term;

- outcomes from teacher assessment and test results;

- sampling pupils' work and achievements across the curriculum;

- focused observations of pupils working in lessons;

- information relating to behaviour, attendance, attitudes to learning, personal and social development, *ECM* outcomes;

- the views of individual pupils in relation to their own progress and how additional provision has helped them to improve their learning and well-being.

Evaluation is concerned with judging the quality, effectiveness, strengths and weaknesses of additional interventions for pupils with SEN/LDD by analysing quantitative and qualitative evidence collected from monitoring. This helps to inform future planning and decision making as to the most effective interventions or teaching and support approaches to utilise with pupils who have SEN/LDD, in order to ensure they make good progress in learning and well-being.

Figure 3.3 provides a template for evaluating the impact of additional provision and interventions delivered by TAs/LSAs and learning mentors from the school staff. Figure 3.4 offers a model for recording the impact of external agencies' inputs.

Ofsted commented on evaluating pupil progress:

> Pupils' achievement – the standards that they reach and their progress – is always at the heart of self-evaluation. It is a key element of the Every Child Matters (ECM) agenda. The school understand how well their pupils are doing because they rigorously track the personal development and academic progress of individuals, particular groups and cohorts of pupils. In this way they identify potential problems at an early stage and act upon them swiftly to counteract underachievement, poor behaviour and unsatisfactory attitudes to learning.
>
> (Ofsted 2006b: 5)

The ongoing evidence that is gathered from teaching, learning and *ECM* well-being feeds into the school's self-evaluation process and the SEF. As a result of this process it is important that trainee and newly qualified teachers and TAs together have the evidence from their monitoring and evaluation to answer the following questions:

- How much are we currently doing towards improving SEN/LDD pupils' learning and well-being?

- How well are we doing it?

- What difference is it making?

- How do we know?

- What have we learnt about removing barriers to learning and participation?

Meeting the Ofsted inspection requirements

September 2009 brought in new Ofsted school inspection arrangements:

- Satisfactory or inadequate schools will be inspected every three years and receive interim monitoring visits from HMI.

Date intervention commenced:	Intervention programme title and length of each session:	Wk 1	Wk 2	Wk 3	Wk 4	Wk 5	Wk 6	Wk 7	Wk 8	Wk 9	Wk 10	Date when intervention programme ceased:	Evaluation of the intervention programme
Pupil name	Attainment at start of intervention:	✓ or X	✓ or X	✓ or X	✓ or X	✓ or X	✓ or X	✓ or X	✓ or X	✓ or X	✓ or X	Attainment at end of intervention:	Evidence of impact

(✓ = attended session; X = absent from session)

Figure 3.3 Template for monitoring and evaluating additional school intervention programmes for SEN/LDD pupils

Nature of interventions and support for *ECM*	Impact on Be healthy	Impact on Stay safe	Impact on Enjoy and achieve	Impact on Make a positive contribution	Impact on Achieve economic well-being

Practitioner/staff name: _____ Service: _____ Date: _____

Figure 3.4 Evaluating the impact of additional interventions and support on pupils' *Every Child Matters* well-being outcomes

From Rita Cheminais (2010), *Special Educational Needs for Newly Qualified Teachers and Teaching Assistants*, 2nd edn. London: Routledge. © 2010 Rita Cheminais

- Good or outstanding schools will be inspected every six years, but will have an Ofsted health check every three years.

- Greater account is to be taken of the views of parents and pupils in relation to the school's contribution to the *Every Child Matters* (*ECM*) outcomes.

- There is to be an increased focus on the progress made by different groups of pupils, e.g. those most likely to underachieve; the most vulnerable; the most able.

- The well-being of learners, the quality of learning and the quality of teaching feature strongly in the revised inspection process.

- Some inspections may have a specific focus, e.g. looked after children, SEN/LDD.

- The criteria for outstanding and good judgements are more explicit.

- Standards for satisfactory and inadequate schools are more clearly defined.

- Senior managers are to be more consistently involved in the school's inspection, e.g. by shadowing and undertaking joint lesson observations with inspectors.

- Greater account will be taken of the capacity of the school to improve.

- More explicit reporting will be given on whether the school provides good value for money.

- Partnerships or federations of schools inspections will be better co-ordinated.

- The school inspection report will include a letter to parents in addition to the letter to pupils.

In the revised inspection process Ofsted will continue to report on:

- the quality of education provided in the school;

- how far the education provided in the school meets the needs of the range of children and young people attending the school;

- the educational standards achieved in the school;

- the quality and effectiveness of the school's leadership and management in ensuring that teaching is consistently effective and has a positive impact on pupils' learning;

- equality, diversity and community cohesion;

- whether the views of parents, children and young people are listened to and acted upon;

- whether the curriculum meets the needs of all learners;

- whether resources are adequate and used well;

- whether all learners are supported effectively;

- the spiritual, moral, social and cultural development of the pupils;

- the contribution made by the school to the well-being of its pupils.

Trainee and newly qualified teachers and TAs need to ensure that:

- lessons are well prepared and the effective deployment of TAs is clear;

- they can demonstrate the impact of teaching and support on pupils' learning;

- pupils make progress and attain the standards they should;

- pupils enjoy their learning because teaching is inspiring and motivating;

- pupils' views are valued and they are involved in reviewing their own progress;
- pupil well-being is promoted appropriately;
- any attendance issues existing among pupils are addressed;
- pupils' behaviour is well managed.

Tim Key (2009), an adviser to the Chief HMI, considered that the best teachers are those who are willing to take risks by delivering creative lessons in a range of styles.

Table 3.5 provides a useful checklist for teachers and teaching assistants in relation to what good and outstanding practice looks like in the classroom.

Table 3.5

Evaluating pupils' progress in learning, behaviour and well-being

Ofsted judgement	Teaching and learning	Behaviour	*ECM* well-being
Outstanding	All learners make considerably better progress than might be expected as a result of very good teaching. Teaching is based upon an expert knowledge of the curriculum and is stimulating and rigorous. Work is sensitively matched to the needs of individuals and high expectations ensure that all learners are challenged and stretched whatever standard they are working at. Teaching methods are imaginatively selected to deliver the objectives of the lesson. Assessment of learners' work successfully underpins the teaching and learners have a clear idea of how to improve. No time is wasted in the lesson. Teaching assistants and resources are very well directed to support learning.	Learners' behaviour is mature and thoughtful and contributes to successful learning. Learners are very supportive of each other in lessons. Learners show great consideration for each other. Learners behave very well and are engrossed in their work. Excellent pupil relationships are conducive to their personal development.	Care, guidance and support for learners is very good and exemplary. Learners' self-confidence and self-esteem is very good and they have high aspirations. Learners feel very safe. Learners have a high level of involvement in community activities. Learners' views are central to school decision making. Learners' financial literacy is very good. Learners enjoyment of learning and school is very high.
Good	Most learners including those with LDD make good progress and show good attitudes to their work, as a result of good effective teaching. Learners are keen to get on with their work. Very good use is made of ICT.	Behaviour overall is good and any unsatisfactory behaviour is managed effectively. Learners' behaviour makes a strong contribution to good learning in lessons. Their behaviour is welcoming and positive.	Learners work in a safe, secure and friendly environment. The health and safety of learners is not endangered in any way. Pupils are learning to understand their feelings.

Table 3.5 continued

Evaluating pupils' progress in learning, behaviour and well-being

Ofsted judgement	Teaching and learning	Behaviour	*ECM* well-being
Good (continued)	Teaching is well informed, confident, engaging and precise.	Learners show responsibility in responding to routine expectations, set consistent standards for themselves and need only rare guidance from staff about how to conduct themselves.	All learners enjoy school a great deal.
	Teachers' good subject knowledge lends confidence to teaching styles which engage learners and encourage them to become independent learners.	Learners behave well towards each other, showing respect and encouraging others to conduct themselves equally well.	Learners feel safe, are safety conscious without being fearful, and they adopt healthy lifestyles.
	Work is well matched and tailored to the full range of learners' needs, so that most are suitably challenged.	Learners demonstrate considerate behaviour, positive attitudes and regular attendance.	Learners develop a commitment to racial equality.
	The level of challenge stretches learners without inhibiting.		Learners make good overall progress in developing the personal qualities that enable them to contribute effectively to the community and eventually to transfer to later working life.
	Teaching methods are effectively related to the lesson objectives and the needs of learners.		Learners have good opportunities to contribute to and take on responsibilities in the community.
	Learners are gaining knowledge, skills and understanding at a good rate across all key stages. Learning is good in the majority of subjects and courses.		Learners are well prepared for their future economic well-being.
	The response of different groups of learners to the curriculum is carefully monitored.		Effective strategies exist for promoting learners' social and economic well-being.
	Assessment of learners' work is regular and consistent and it makes a good contribution to their progress.		Teaching styles and available activities effectively promote learners' enterprising qualities.
	Accurate assessment informs learners how to improve.		
	Learners are guided to assess their own work.		
	Enrichment opportunities are good.		
	Teaching assistants and resources are well deployed and directed to support learning.		
	Good relationships support parents and carers in helping to succeed.		

Useful resources relating to assessment, monitoring and evaluation

Web-based resources

The National Strategies website has a range of information and resources on assessment in the primary and secondary phase. AfL and APP are both featured. The website is at http://nationalstrategies.standards.dcsf.gov.uk/

Teachers TV offers a range of Teachers TV videos on assessment in the primary phase and the secondary phase, which can be viewed or downloaded from the website http://www.teachers.tv/assessment

Teachers TV has a range of Teachers TV videos on Ofsted inspections in the primary and secondary phase, including preparing for the inspection. These can be viewed or downloaded at http://www.teachers.tv/search/node/Ofsted+inspections

Information about RAISEonline can be obtained from the website http://www.raiseonline.org

Leading on Inclusion (DfES 2005a), the second part of *Understanding and Using Data* is a resource for the primary phase of education, focusing particularly on SEN. This DfES resource is available to download from the national strategies website: http://nationalstrategies.standards.dcsf.gov.uk/node/123017 It was sent to every local authority as a hard copy with accompanying CD.

Maximising Progress – Ensuring the Attainment of Pupils with Special Educational Needs, a Key Stage 3 resource, is in three parts: *Part 1 Using data – target setting and target getting*; *Part 2 Approaches to learning and teaching in the mainstream classroom*; *Part 3 Managing the learning process for pupils with SEN*. It can be downloaded from http://www.standards.dfes.gov.uk/secondary/keystge3/all/respub/sen_inc

Questions for reflection

1 Identify three SEN pupils whom you teach or support and indicate how you could improve one aspect of their assessment for learning.

2 How could you extend SEN/LDD pupils' involvement in assessing, recording and reviewing their own progress?

3 How is assessment for learning supporting the improvement of SEN/LDD pupils' learning?

4 How will you make best use of the evidence of the impact of your teaching on improving SEN/LDD pupils' learning and well-being?

5 How are you using and sharing the tracking information relating to SEN/LDD pupil progress in learning and well-being with them?

6 How are you developing the skills to know what progress to expect from pupils with SEN/LDD?

7 What evidence do you have about the impact of the additional personalised interventions on improving the attainment and well-being of SEN/LDD pupils?

8 How useful has RAISEonline been in helping you to analyse and judge whether SEN/LDD pupils are making good progress?

9 How will you ensure that the targets you set for pupils with SEN/LDD have a realistic and appropriate level of challenge?

CHAPTER 4

Developing constructive professional partnerships for collaboration and team working

This chapter will cover:

- Professional and occupational standards for teachers and TAs in their work with colleagues
- Effective partnership with teaching assistants
- Productive partnership with parents/carers of pupils with SEN
- The joint inter-professional values statement for inter-professional working
- Good practice principles for work with colleagues from multi-agencies
- Protocols for information sharing and confidentiality
- Engaging with *Every Child Matters* systems and procedures
- The role of the Special Educational Needs Co-ordinator
- The role and responsibilities of practitioners working with SEN/LDD pupils
- The role of the school improvement partner and SEN, disability and *ECM*
- The role of the Advanced Skills Teacher/Excellent Teacher for SEN
- The role of the local authority SEN and Inclusion Consultant
- Useful resources to support collaborative work with other practitioners
- Further activities

Professional and occupational standards for teachers and TAs in their work with colleagues

The term colleagues is used to refer to all those professionals/practitioners with whom a teacher or teaching assistant (TA) might work. It includes, for example, other teaching and learning support staff in school, the wider workforce in an educational setting, and all those external professionals from health, social services, education, voluntary and community sector organisations, who work directly with pupils and their families. See Table 4.1 for the requirements.

Table 4.1

National standards for teachers and TAs relating to collaborative working

QTS standards	NQT induction standards	NOS for teaching assistants
Communicating and working with others Q4 Communicate effectively with children, young people, colleagues, parents/carers Q5 Recognise and respect the contribution that colleagues, parents/carers can make to the development and well-being of children and young people, and to raising their levels of attainment Q6 Have a commitment to collaboration and co-operative working **Personal professional development** Q9 Act upon advice and feedback and be open to coaching and mentoring **Achievement and diversity** Q20 Know and understand the roles of colleagues with specific responsibilities, including those with responsibility for learners with SEND and other individual learning needs **Health and well-being** Q21 (b) Know how to identify and support children and young people whose progress, development or well-being is affected by changes or difficulties in their personal circumstances, and when to refer them to colleagues for specialist support **Team working and collaboration** Q32 Work as a team member and identify opportunities for working with colleagues, sharing the development of effective practice with them	**1 Developing professional and constructive relationships** C4 (a) Communicate effectively with children, young people and colleagues C6 Have a commitment to collaboration and co-operative working where appropriate C40 Work as a team member and identify opportunities for working with colleagues, managing their work where appropriate, and sharing the development of effective practice with them C41 Ensure that colleagues working with them are appropriately involved in supporting learning and understand the roles they are expected to fulfil **2 Working within the law and frameworks** C21 Know when to draw on the expertise of colleagues, such as those with responsibility for the safeguarding of children and young people and SEND, and to refer to sources of information, advice and support from external agencies **3 Professional knowledge and understanding** **ii Promoting children's and young people's development and well-being** C5 Recognise and respect the contributions that colleagues, parents/carers make to the development and well-being of children and young people, and to raising their levels of attainment C20 Understand the roles of colleagues such as those having specific responsibilities for learners with SEND and other	**NVQ Level 2** STL4 **Contribute to positive relationships** (interacting with and responding positively to children, young people and adults and valuing people equally) STL5 **Provide effective support for your colleagues** (being an effective member of staff; working effectively with colleagues and taking an active role in developing skills and expertise) STL14 **Support individuals during therapy sessions** (supporting therapists and individuals before, during and following therapy sessions; help prepare for the therapy session; support therapy sessions and contribute to the review of therapy sessions) **NVQ Level 3** STL20 **Develop and promote positive relationships** (developing and promoting positive relationships with children and young people; communicating with children/young people and adults; fostering positive relationships between children/young people and with other adults) STL21 **Support the development and effectiveness of work teams** (contribute to team practice; take an active role in supporting and developing team effectiveness)

Table 4.1 continued

National standards for teachers and TAs relating to collaborative working

QTS standards		NQT induction standards		NOS for teaching assistants	
Q33	Ensure that colleagues working with them are appropriately involved in supporting learning and understand the roles they are expected to fulfil		individual learning needs, and the contributions they can make to the learning, development and well-being of children/young people	STL62	**Develop and maintain working relationships with other practitioners** (work effectively with other practitioners by doing what can be done to support their work and using their strengths and expertise to support and develop the individual's working practices and procedures)
		C25	Know how to identify and support children/young people whose progress, development and well-being are affected by changes or difficulties in their personal circumstances, and when to refer them to colleagues for specialist support		
		5 Developing practice			
		C9	Act upon advice and feedback and be open to coaching and mentoring		

Source: TDA (2007a, 2007b, 2007c).

Effective partnership with teaching assistants

Ofsted found that: 'Support by teaching assistants can be vital, but the organisation of it can mean pupils having insufficient opportunity to develop their understanding, skills and independence' (Ofsted 2004: 15).

Ofsted went on to comment in the same report on their inspection findings: 'Given the investment that schools make in teaching assistants to support pupils with SEN, the systems for managing and making use of the intelligence they can provide were surprisingly weak in many schools, particularly in the secondary schools visited' (Ofsted 2004: 20; paragraph 93).

Later, in 2006, in relation to SEN pupils' provision Ofsted reported that: 'Pupils in mainstream schools where support from teaching assistants was the main type of provision were less likely to make good academic progress than those who had access to specialist teaching in those schools' (Ofsted 2006a: 3). Ofsted recommended that mainstream schools should 'analyse critically their use and deployment of teaching assistants' (Ofsted 2006a: 5).

Teaching assistants work with teachers in order to:

- promote the participation of all pupils, including those with SEN/LDD, in the social and academic practices of the school/setting;
- assist in raising the standards and achievement of pupils they support and work with, and encourage pupils to become independent learners.

Teaching assistants' support includes:

- helping with classroom resources and records;
- helping with the care and support of pupils;

- providing support for learning activities;
- providing support for colleagues.

The key role of TAs in the primary phase, and learning LSAs in the secondary phase, is to ensure that SEN/LDD pupils are actively included in lessons and other extra-curricular extended school activities, alongside their peers. In order to make best use of TAs/LSAs, trainee and newly qualified teachers should ensure that:

- they give the TA/LSA copies of the relevant National Curriculum schemes of work, programmes of study and the attainment level descriptors, along with any catch-up intervention materials;
- any intervention work undertaken by TAs/LSAs within and outside the classroom enables pupils to transfer their knowledge and skills across the curriculum;
- any targeted withdrawal work does not preclude the SEN/LDD pupil from inclusion opportunities with their peers or contact with the class/subject teacher;
- the TA/LSA is involved in the planning of lessons and in the differentiation of the curriculum;
- the learning objectives and expected learning outcomes for the lesson are clarified and shared with the TA/LSA;
- the TA/LSA is briefed on their role in the lesson and know how best they can help to support SEN/LDD pupils in making progress;
- quality time is made available to discuss pupil progress with the TA/LSA;
- the TA/LSA is clear about classroom rules and behaviour management.

Table 4.2 provides an overview of the key roles of the TA/LSA working with class/subject teachers in primary and secondary mainstream schools.

Productive partnership with parents/carers of pupils with SEN

Trainee and newly qualified teachers need to be aware that the parents/carers of pupils with SEN/LDD may experience additional pressures and anxieties about their child's education. They may be particularly sensitive or reactive to a teacher's comments about their son's or daughter's slower progress. Clear, sensitive communication and mutual respect are two essential factors necessary in establishing positive relationships between a teacher and parents/carers of a child with SEN/LDD.

Parents/carers are the primary educators of their child. Children spend 87 per cent of their time at home with their parents/carers. The parents/carers of pupils with SEN/LDD may be articulate and over-anxious, readily communicating their concerns about their child's difficulties and lack of progress, while having high expectations. Alternatively, the parents/carers of pupils with SEN/LDD may lack confidence and rarely attend parents' evenings or review meetings at school. They may appear to be unconcerned about their child's progress or behaviour. These parents/carers may have had negative schooling experiences themselves when they were younger.

Table 4.2

The key roles of the TA/LSA

TA/LSA key role	Specific tasks for TA /LSA role
Supporting pupils' personalised learning	• Support pupils' learning activities across the curriculum, tailoring support strategies to match learners' needs • Support pupils to become independent and collaborative learners • Support pupils' learning through the use of ICT and multi-media technology • Utilise accelerated learning approaches to support pupils' learning • Observe, feedback and report on pupil performance and achievements • Support pupils' assessment for learning and APP by helping them to review their own learning and progress • Promote and support inclusion by removing barriers to learning and participation • Prepare learning materials • Support the development and maintenance of a healthy, safe and secure learning environment • Contribute to the planning, delivery and evaluation of teaching activities • Support teaching in a specific curriculum area • Prepare, maintain and use equipment and subject-specific resources to improve pupils' curriculum access • Develop and evaluate materials to support teaching and learning in a curriculum area • Contribute to the monitoring and assessment of pupils' progress in a curriculum area
Meeting additional support needs	• Provide support to pupils with additional needs, which includes gifted and talented pupils (SEN pupils with dual and multiple exceptionalities), as well as those with LDD • Contribute to the management of pupils' behaviour, supporting them to take responsibility for their own behaviour • Provide support for literacy and numeracy to enhance wider curriculum access • Support the delivery of targeted interventions and programmes for literacy and numeracy, feeding back to teachers on the impact on pupils' progress and *ECM* well-being outcomes
Providing pastoral support for pupil well-being	• Act as a learning guide/key adult to targeted vulnerable pupils • Promote and support pupils' well-being and resilience, helping them to form positive and productive relationships with others • Promote and support the development of pupils' emotional literacy • Support pupils to cope with change during transfer and transition
Supporting the wider work of the school	• Comply with school policies and procedures related to child protection and safeguarding children; health and safety; confidentiality, information sharing and data protection; *Every Child Matters*; equal opportunities; and inclusion • Escort and supervise pupils on educational visits, undertaking out-of-school activities, extended school activities • Contribute information to the CAF process • Support teachers in the administration of tests and examinations • Contribute to maintaining pupil records • Provide admin support to teachers, e.g. photocopying, collecting dinner money, filing • Contribute to the school's self-evaluation and school improvement processes • Assist with the display of learners' work and achievements

Table 4.2 continued

The key roles of the TA/LSA

TA/LSA key role	Specific tasks for TA/LSA role
Working with colleagues/other practitioners	• Mediate between pupils, teachers and other professionals to support and develop pupils' learning and well-being • Support and maintain productive, collaborative partnerships and working relationships with other frontline workers from external agencies and with school colleagues • Support and contribute to the development and effectiveness of team work • Provide active support for other colleagues • Take an active part in developing your own continuing professional development and maintain a portfolio of evidence to support annual appraisal review

Key principles for working in partnership with parents/carers

- Acknowledge and draw upon parents'/carers' knowledge and experience about their child, as they can offer useful insights and valuable information.

- Begin a discussion by focusing on the pupil's strengths and achievements.

- Recognise the feelings and emotions of parents with SEN pupils – they experience feelings of guilt.

- Go through any documentation or particular SEN procedures with the parents/carers of SEN pupils to prevent any misunderstandings.

- Actively listen to what the parents/carers tell you about their child's learning and behaviour.

- Ensure you communicate with parents/carers of SEN pupils using their preferred method, e.g. email, telephone, face-to-face meeting, letter.

- Keep parents/carers informed about the progress and behaviour of their child in your class.

- View parents positively as essential partners in their child's education.

- Signpost parents/carers to further support and advice as appropriate; for example, they may welcome their child being able to access a homework club or extended school activities.

Further tips for working with parents/carers

- Prepare well in advance for any meetings with parents/carers.

- If you think a meeting is going to run over the set time, arrange a future meeting with the parents/carers.

- Offer parents/carers practical strategies for supporting their child's learning, behaviour and well-being at home.

- Encourage parents/carers to attend any family learning sessions, where relevant.

- Respond to any parental issues or queries promptly.

- Ensure any written reports to parents/carers are clear and concise, and avoid using too much jargon or comment banks.

The joint inter-professional values statement for inter-professional working

In 2007 the General Teaching Council for England (GTC), the Nursing and Midwifery Council (NMC) and the General Social Care Council (GSCC) agreed upon a joint statement of inter-professional values underpinning work with children and young people. These inter-professional values for work with colleagues are reflected in the Professional Standards for Teachers, in the Induction Standards for NQTs and in the National Occupational Standards for Supporting Teaching and Learning in Schools. Trainee and newly qualified teachers and TAs would be well advised to ensure they take note of and apply the inter-professional values for working with children, young people and other colleagues to their everyday practice. It would be good practice for NQTs and TAs to record in their portfolio of professional development the significant contributions that they and other colleagues have made which have helped to further their knowledge, skills and expertise in relation to collaborative partnership to improve learning and well-being outcomes for SEND pupils. Table 4.3 provides an overview of some of the key inter-professional values that are most relevant to newly qualified and trainee teachers/TAs when working with colleagues. Figure 4.1 records collaborative working.

Good practice principles for work with colleagues from multi-agencies

In order to ensure work in collaborative partnership with multi-agency practitioners is effective, it is useful for newly qualified teachers and TAs to follow ten key principles.

1 Know the roles of the multi-agency practitioners who work directly with pupils with SEN/LDD and additional educational needs (AEN).

2 Ensure multi-agency practitioners are clear about your role.

3 Understand the law and frameworks relating to SEN, disability and *ECM*.

Table 4.3

Joint statement of inter-professional values for working with other colleagues, most relevant to NQTs and TAs new to their role

Statement descriptors of values for inter-professional work with other colleagues
● Children's practitioners value the contribution that a range of colleagues make to children's lives, and they form effective relationships across the children's workforce. Their inter-professional practice is based on a willingness to bring their own expertise to bear on the pursuit of shared goals for children, and a respect for the expertise of others.
● Practitioners involved in inter-professional work recognise the need to be clear about lines of communication, management and accountability as these may be more complex than in their specialist setting.
● Children's practitioners understand that the knowledge, understanding and skills for inter-professional work may differ from those in their own specialism and they are committed to professional learning in this area as well as in their own field, through training and engagement with research and other evidence.
● They are committed to reflecting on and improving their inter-professional practice, and to applying their inter-professional learning to their specialist work with children.
● Work with children can be emotionally demanding, and children's practitioners are sensitive to and supportive of each other's well-being.

Source: GTC (2007: 1).

Joint inter-professional statement aspects	Key tasks and significant contributions	Other practitioners working with you	New knowledge, skills and expertise learned	Impact of collaborative partnership working
Value and respect the contributions of other colleagues				
Be willing to use own expertise in pursuit of shared goals				
Follow clear lines of communication, management and accountability				
Be willing to learn from other colleagues through training and engagement with research				
Commit to reflecting on and improving own inter-professional practice and apply inter-professional learning to work with SEND pupils				
Be sensitive to and supportive of other colleagues' well-being				

Figure 4.1 Making a difference through collaborative work

From Rita Cheminais (2010), *Special Educational Needs for Newly Qualified Teachers and Teaching Assistants*, 2nd edn. London: Routledge. © 2010 Rita Cheminais

4 Know the procedures and protocols for making a service referral, obtaining an assessment and securing further specialist interventions for pupils.

5 Utilise the correct channels of communication for information sharing and be aware of confidentiality issues.

6 Understand the professional language and terminology used by multi-agency practitioners.

7 Have realistic expectations about what can be achieved through collaborative partnership in a given timescale.

8 Respect and value equally the contributions of other practitioners who work with pupils with SEN/LDD/AEN.

9 Make time to meet with multi-agency practitioners to discuss and review the impact of interventions for targeted SEN/LDD/AEN pupils.

10 Know who to refer to in the school/setting if you have any queries or issues about any aspect of multi-agency partnership working.

Protocols for information sharing and confidentiality

The appropriate sharing of information is important because it ensures that children and young people with additional needs get the services they require in order to achieve the five *Every Child Matters (ECM)* outcomes.

The Data Protection Act 1998 provides a legal framework for sharing information lawfully and professionally among children's workforce practitioners. Before information is shared between school staff and multi-agency practitioners in the children's workforce, it is useful to refer to the DCSF seven golden rules for information sharing which are as follows:

1 **Remember that the Data Protection Act is not a barrier to sharing information** but provides a framework to ensure that personal information about living persons is shared appropriately.

2 **Be open and honest** with the child concerned (and/or their family where appropriate) from the outset about why, what, how and with whom information will or could be shared, and seek their agreement, unless it is unsafe or inappropriate to do so.

3 **Seek advice** if you are in any doubt, where possible without disclosing the identity of the child concerned.

4 **Share with consent where appropriate** and, where possible, respect the wishes of those who do not consent to share confidential information. You may still share information without consent if, in your judgement, the lack of consent can be overridden in the public interest. You will need to base your judgements on the facts of the case.

5 **Consider safety and well-being**. Base your information-sharing decisions on considerations of the safety and well-being of the child concerned and others who may be affected by their actions.

6 **Necessary, proportionate, relevant, accurate, timely and secure**: ensure that the information you share is necessary for the purpose for which you are sharing

it, is shared only with those people who need to have it, is accurate and up to date, is shared in a timely fashion, and is shared securely.

7 **Keep a record** of your decision and the reasons for it – whether it is to share information or not. If you decide to share, then record what you have shared, with whom and for what purpose (DCSF 2008d: 4–5).

Confidentiality

Information is confidential if it is sensitive, not already in the public domain, or given to you in the expectation that it will not be shared with others. Confidential information can be shared if you have the consent of the person who provided the information or the person to whom the information relates. Confidential information can be shared without consent if there is an overwhelming 'public interest', e.g. to prevent significant harm to a child or others; to prevent a serious crime; or when you are ordered to do so by a court. Consent to share information must be informed, e.g. the person giving consent needs to understand why information needs to be shared, who will see their information, the purpose to which it will be put and the implications of sharing that information. A young person is able to give consent in their own right, irrespective of age, as long as they have sufficient understanding about what sharing information means.

The education setting you work in should have a 'need to know' policy in operation, relating to information sharing and confidentiality. Such a policy makes the following explicit:

- what information is required;
- under what circumstances the information can be released;
- to whom it is appropriate to release the information;
- how the information will be used;
- how the released information will be crucial to improving outcomes for the child or young person concerned;
- when written consent is required for the release of information;
- all confidential conversations about children/young people and their families must take place in a private sound-proofed office;
- all staff must know about ContactPoint.

Engaging with *Every Child Matters* systems and procedures

The aim of *ECM*, through its systems and procedures as outlined in the Children Act 2004, is to integrate services for children and young people from birth to age 19, in order to support more effective prevention and early intervention. It is estimated that at any one time, three to four million children and young people will need additional services.

ContactPoint and the Common Assessment Framework (CAF) are two key elements of the *ECM* strategy that newly qualified and experienced teachers/TAs in particular are likely to come across in their work in schools. Both are concerned with getting co-ordinated help moving quickly for targeted and specialist services.

In terms of *ECM* procedures, NQTs and TAs may be requested by a lead professional (LP) from within or outside school to provide information about a child's/young person's learning and well-being which will contribute to the CAF process, and may also inform discussion about provision for the child and their family at a team around the child (TAC) meeting.

Each of these systems and procedures will be described in turn in order to enable trainee and newly qualified teachers and TAs to gain a better understanding about them.

ContactPoint

ContactPoint is a national basic electronic information-sharing system, designed to help frontline services work together more effectively in order to meet the needs of children, young people and their families. It is a quick way to find out who else is working with the same child or young person, thus making it easier to deliver more co-ordinated support and services, and so avoid duplication of work across services.

This basic online directory is only available to authorised staff, and in school this is likely to be the SENCO. Other authorised users include practitioners from education, early years and child care services, Connexions, health, social care, youth offending services, police and the voluntary sector. Around 330,000 authorised practitioners are likely to use ContactPoint. Each must have obtained an enhanced CRB certificate valid for at least three years. ContactPoint contains the following basic information:

- name, address, gender, date of birth and unique identifying number of all children and young people in England up to the age of 18;
- name and contact details of parents and carers, educational setting, GP and other services working with the child;
- the name of the lead professional (if there is one), and if a CAF has been completed.

The information that can be held on ContactPoint is limited by law, as stated in Section 12 of the Children Act 2004 and by the supporting regulations which came into force on 1 August 2007. These regulations stipulate that any case information is prohibited from ContactPoint.

The advantage of ContactPoint is that it facilitates communication across services, as soon as a first sign of need is noticed. ContactPoint will be automatically updated with information. Once a child reaches 18, unless they have learning difficulties that make them vulnerable as adults, the information is removed from ContactPoint. It is retained for six years in a safe archive and subsequently destroyed after that time.

Parents can ask the LA ContactPoint management team if they can access the information about their child in ContactPoint. If the child is 12 or over, the right of access to the information belongs to him or her. The LA is under no obligation to disclose ContactPoint information to a parent for safeguarding reasons. ContactPoint became fully operational nationally in early 2009.

The Common Assessment Framework

The CAF adopts a holistic approach to the assessment of a child's/young person's additional needs, if they are not being met by universal services, and they are not achieving well on the *ECM* outcomes. The CAF facilitates joined-up co-ordinated working between services.

The CAF form provides a common assessment across services to enable the practitioners to decide how best to meet a child's/young person's additional needs. It also supports swift and easy access to targeted and specialist services such as speech and language therapy, sexual health advice and support, and Child and Adolescent Mental Health Services (CAMHS) and special educational needs and disability services.

The CAF also enables school staff to establish quick links with multi-agency practitioners, helping to remove barriers to learning and improve children's and young people's well-being. Schools need to ensure that all members of staff:

- are clear about their role in the early identification of emerging emotional distress and health needs in pupils;
- know where they can get support from a local multi-agency team;
- have access to information about services available in their local area;
- understand their legal responsibilities in relation to safeguarding, child protection, special educational needs and disability;
- understand when, why and how a CAF can be used, and how to feed information into the CAF;
- know how to use the CAF pre-assessment checklist which can also accompany the Foundation Stage Profile and other assessments for older children and young people;
- utilise the expertise within their own school from practitioners on site, e.g. the SENCO, school nurse, learning mentor, pastoral leaders and EWO.

Staff who have to complete a full CAF, in particular lead professionals, will have had training in how to fill in the CAF form. An eCAF is also available which allows authorised practitioners to have access to CAF information electronically.

Figure 4.2 shows the CAF pre-assessment checklist which provides a useful point of reference to NQTs and TAs new to their role. The CAF pre-assessment checklist, like the full CAF form, links to the five *ECM* well-being outcomes. Teachers and TAs will have considerable information to put into the CAF in relation to sections on learning and health.

The CAF forms and guide to definitions can be downloaded from the website www.everychildmatters.gov.uk/deliveringservices/caf/

Team around the child

The TAC facilitates effective multi-agency working to improve outcomes for vulnerable children and young people through integrated support from all services involved with the family. Practitioners from the same and different services work closely together to meet the unmet needs of the child or young person. The child/young person is fully involved in all decisions about the help and services they require. The services take into account the family's priorities, their values and cultural background. Problems and solutions are addressed in a holistic way, through an agreed written action plan which clarifies each TAC member's responsibilities.

The TAC comprises a small, sharply focused team of practitioners. It may include, for example, the SENCO or a learning mentor, an educational psychologist, a health visitor and a social worker. The composition of the team is dependent on the needs of the child/young person, and its members may vary as the child's/young person's needs change over time.

Name of pupil: _____ Date of birth: _____ Form/Class: _____

ECM outcome/aspect	Yes	No	Not sure	Comments
Does the pupil appear to be healthy?	☐	☐	☐	_____ _____ _____ _____ _____
Is the pupil safe from harm?	☐	☐	☐	_____ _____ _____ _____ _____
Is the pupil learning and developing?	☐	☐	☐	_____ _____ _____ _____ _____
Is the pupil having a positive impact on others?	☐	☐	☐	_____ _____ _____ _____ _____
Is the pupil free from the negative impact of poverty?	☐	☐	☐	_____ _____ _____ _____ _____

Name of practitioner: _____

Job: _____

Date completed this pre-assessment checklist: _____

Figure 4.2 Pre-assessment CAF checklist

From Rita Cheminais (2010), *Special Educational Needs for Newly Qualified Teachers and Teaching Assistants*, 2nd edn. London: Routledge. © 2010 Rita Cheminais

The advantage of the TAC is that because it is multi–agency, it will have a wide range of skills and expertise that will help to address and solve problems more effectively through collaboration. NQTs and TAs may be required to contribute information about a child's/young person's learning and well-being, which will help to inform future action and provision.

Example of CAF and TAC in action

The class teacher has noticed that Courtney has started arriving late for school; she is having occasional days off school each week; she is not getting on with her peers and loses her temper very quickly; her school work has become untidy, incomplete, and homework is not being given in. She is reported not to be eating her school lunch. When asked by her class teacher if there is anything worrying her she says there is nothing wrong. Courtney is not achieving very well in relation to the *Every Child Matters* outcomes.

The class teacher meets with the SENCO and the *Every Child Matters* (*ECM*) Manager in school. The SENCO checks ContactPoint to see if there is any information about Courtney. There is nothing to indicate that any other services are working with Courtney.

The *ECM* Manager contacts Courtney's mother to ask her to meet her and the class teacher to discuss her daughter's recent behaviour in school. At the meeting with Courtney's mother it is recommended that a CAF form is completed. Courtney's mother informs the *ECM* Manager and the class teacher that her husband has left her and moved out of the house. She also indicates that Courtney's behaviour has been difficult to manage at home since her husband's departure. Courtney's mother gives permission for the class teacher and the *ECM* Manager to complete a CAF form. The completed CAF is submitted electronically to the local authority.

The *ECM* Manager calls a multi-agency meeting and invites the Education Welfare Officer, the School Nurse, the BEST teacher from the LA and a Social Worker to join her, the class teacher and the SENCO at the meeting. The *ECM* Manager is identified as the lead professional. She chairs the multi-agency meeting and Courtney's mother attends. A CAF action plan identifies all the support, interventions and additional service provision that will be needed to meet Courtney's needs. Each practitioner agrees upon the support and interventions they will deliver. A date for a review meeting in six weeks' time is agreed upon, when Courtney's progress will be evaluated.

The class teacher works in partnership with the BEST teacher to address Courtney's behaviour, self-esteem and social skills issues. The BEST teacher supports Courtney's mother with useful strategies to help her manage her daughter's behaviour at home. The school nurse provides advice to Courtney on healthy eating and monitors her lunchtime eating habits. The social worker provides counselling support to Courtney and her mother to help them cope without the father/husband. The SENCO organises some after-school activities for Courtney and she attends the homework club and the games club. The SENCO also agrees to provide in-class support from a teaching assistant, who already works with the class group. The Education Welfare Officer supports Courtney's mother in ensuring her daughter attends school.

After six weeks the multi-agency meeting reviews Courtney's progress and there have been good improvements in her behaviour, attendance, punctuality, attitudes to learning, self-esteem and social skills. Her mother reports that her daughter's behaviour has improved greatly at home and Courtney is willing to help her mother more in the home.

The class teacher agrees to monitor Courtney for the rest of the term. She agrees that no further additional support and interventions are required at present, but she will call on the other practitioners if they need to be recommenced. Courtney's mother is happy with the decision, and Courtney has been grateful for the support and now feels she can cope alone.

The lead professional

The LP is key to the team around the child. Their role is to:

- co-ordinate the service delivery of the agreed CAF action plan;
- act as a single point of contact for the child/young person and their family;
- monitor and communicate progress on the CAF action plan to all parties, including the family;
- call any necessary multi-agency meetings and record any changes or amendments to the CAF action plan;
- act as a gatekeeper for information sharing;
- deliver their own part of the CAF action plan.

Any frontline practitioner working with vulnerable children and their families can be a lead professional. Whoever the lead professional is, the child/young person and their family must trust and feel confident in working with them. The lead professional is the adult who has the most frequent and regular contact with the child/young person and their family. Lead professionals will usually come from health, social care or education services. However, the lead professional may also come from the staff in a school. They may be the SENCO or learning mentor, or a pastoral leader. The lead professional may change as the needs of the child/young person change over time.

The role of the special educational needs co-ordinator

The SENCO is a vital point of contact for all trainee and newly qualified teachers and teaching assistants. They have a wealth of experience, skills and knowledge in working with pupils with SEN/LDD. The SENCO's key responsibilities are as follows:

- to inform parents/carers that their child has SEN and is on the school's SEN register;
- to identify pupils' special educational needs;
- to co-ordinate SEN provision for SEN pupils to meet their needs;
- to monitor the effectiveness of SEN provision made for SEN pupils;
- to secure relevant services for SEN pupils where necessary;
- to maintain and keep up-to-date records on SEN pupils and the SEN provision made to meet those needs;
- on a regular basis to liaise with, and provide information to, the parents/carers of pupils with SEN;

- to ensure all relevant information about a pupil's SEN and SEN provision made to meet those needs is conveyed to the next school or educational institution on transfer and transition;

- to promote the inclusion of SEN pupils in the school community, the curriculum, facilities and extra-curricular activities;

- to recruit, supervise and train LSAs/TAs who work with SEN pupils;

- to advise teachers at the school about the differentiated teaching methods appropriate to individual pupils with SEN;

- to contribute to in-service training for teachers at the school to assist them to meet the needs of pupils with SEN;

- to prepare and review the information required to be published by the governing body in making provision for SEN and the SEN policy.

The SENCO will input into the induction programme for newly qualified teachers and TAs new to their role. This input will cover:

- clarifying the role of the SENCO;

- familiarisation with the school's SEN and inclusion policy and provision;

- providing advice on IEPs and GEPs;

- providing a guide to SEN/LDD terminology and abbreviations;

- signposts to further sources of information and resources, as well as helping to learn from external practitioners such as the EP and therapists;

- arranging visits to special schools and mainstream schools with resourced SEN provision;

- providing demonstration lessons on how to meet the needs of SEN pupils in the classroom;

- providing advice and guidance on curriculum differentiation, quality-first teaching and waves of intervention for pupils with SEN/LDD;

- providing advice on the effective deployment of TAs and other supporting adults;

- providing information on using smaller stepped assessment such as the P scales.

Figure 4.3 provides a model audit to help trainee and newly qualified teachers and TAs to identify their training needs, as part of their continuing professional development programme, in relation to SEND. Figure 4.3 is an example of a typical SEN CPD audit.

The role and responsibilities of practitioners working with SEN/LDD pupils

Table 4.4 provides a useful summary of the key roles undertaken by a range of different members of the children's workforce who support and work with pupils who have additional needs, including SEN and disability.

Their core purpose is to remove barriers to learning and participation, and to improve the *ECM* well-being outcomes of the children and young people they work with. They work collaboratively with other colleagues/practitioners from within and outside the school, to ensure those with additional needs reach their optimum potential.

Name: _____ **Role:** _____

Please tick the following aspects related to SEN and disability that you feel you require further training and information in.

1   Identifying a diversity of SEN/LDD ☐

2   Managing pupil behaviour ☐

3   Differentiating the curriculum ☐

4   Personalised learning approaches for SEN/LDD pupils ☐

5   Assessing and tracking SEN/LDD pupil progress ☐

6   Implementing meaningful IEPs/GEPs ☐

7   Target setting for pupils with SEN/LDD ☐

8   Quality-first teaching for pupils with SEN/LDD ☐

9   Waves of interventions for pupils with SEN/LDD ☐

10 How to work collaboratively with other colleagues/practitioners ☐

11 Monitoring and evaluating the impact of SEN provision on pupils' outcomes ☐

12 Understanding and using the P scales and EBD scales ☐

Any other training needs for SEN and disability, not included in the list above, that you would like:

_____

_____

_____

_____

Thank you for completing this audit.

Please return your completed SEN and disability audit to the SENCO.

Figure 4.3 SEN/LDD audit for trainee and newly qualified teachers and TAs

From Rita Cheminais (2010), *Special Educational Needs for Newly Qualified Teachers and Teaching Assistants*, 2nd edn. London: Routledge. © 2010 Rita Cheminais

Table 4.4

Roles of key practitioners working with SEND pupils in schools

Learning mentor	Social care worker	School nurse	Educational psychologist
• Help pupils engage more effectively in learning via individual and small group support	• Rapid response case work	• Provide confidential advice and guidance on a range of health-related issues including nutrition, exercise, smoking, mental health, drug abuse, sexual health	• Undertake therapeutic work with children and their parents
• Provide support and interventions to enable pupils to manage their behaviour and emotions, e.g. anger management, conflict resolution, peer mediation	• Parents/carers and family support, e.g. parent drop-ins, family learning classes	• Promote good health and support children and young people to make healthy life choices	• Early identification of problems and early intervention
• Help to reduce exclusions	• Support transition from nursery to primary and from primary to secondary school	• Contribute to the school's PSHE programme and the Healthy Schools initiative	• Engage in action research to promote increased teacher knowledge of good inclusive practice, and raise expectations
• Provide direct support and guidance to pupils on study skills, personal organisation, revision and exam techniques	• Anger management	• Help to develop and update the school's health and safety policy and the sex education policy	• Engage in projects to raise pupil achievement and improve provision for BESD pupils
• Implement programmes of support to prevent bullying	• Support the CAF process	• Provide advice on healthy school meals, and access to drinking water for pupils	• Support the professional development of teachers, TAs, and contribute to governor training
• Provide motivational programmes to raise pupils' aspirations, improve their confidence and build their self-esteem and resilience	• Support the school's PSHE programme	• Contribute to the school's extended services provision by running an after-school healthy eating cookery club	• Work collaboratively with other multi-agency practitioners
• Work in partnership with multi-agency practitioners such as EWOs to improve attendance	• Signposting to specialist services	• Provide a drop-in clinic for children, young people and their parents on or near the school site	• Support parents/carers as key partners in their child's learning and well-being
• Liaise and work with parents; deliver workshops on parenting skills, family learning and managing their child's behaviour	• Counselling and mentoring	• Support individual pupils with long-term medical needs health plans	• Promote a solution-oriented approach to problem solving in relation to pupil learning, behaviour and well-being
• Run breakfast clubs and homework clubs	• Relationship building between schools and families	• Support the safeguarding work of the school by advising staff	• Work with individual children and young people who have severe, complex and challenging needs
• Support pupil transitions	• Group and one-to-one support for children and young people	• Provide immunisation to pupils where appropriate	• Involvement in the statutory assessment of children with the most complex needs, e.g. SEN
• Support and train pupil mentors	• Pupil support for bereavement, self-esteem, behaviour and attendance, depression, self-harming, school anxiety/phobia, family violence, substance abuse, bullying, suicidal threats	• Run parent groups	• Monitor and evaluate the impact of EP interventions and training on improving pupils' *ECM* outcomes
• Support and assist school staff in dealing with difficult pupil incidents	• Act as an advocate for children, young people and their families		
	• Deliver workshops and seminars to teachers and other school staff, related to social-emotional and risk issues such as: how to manage pupils' behaviour in the classroom		
	• Help to identify school staff and other agency practitioners who can help to maximise pupil success		

Table 4.4 continued

Roles of key practitioners working with SEND pupils in schools

Education welfare officer	Speech and language therapist	Connexions personal adviser	LA SEN outreach teacher
• Support schools in improving pupils' attendance	• Assess children's communication needs	• Offer one-to-one support, advice and guidance to pupils aged 13 to 19 on careers, training and employment opportunities	• Provide advice and support on assessing pupils' needs
• Undertake targeted individual and group case work	• Provide direct specialist speech therapy sessions to individual and small groups of children	• Act as an advocate and mediator for young people, particularly those with SEND or who are vulnerable, by offering advice about more specialist services and organisations	• Undertake team teaching, coaching and mentoring class teachers.
• Protect children from the risks of exploitation and harm, e.g. child employment	• Provide training to teachers and support, assistants in delivering speech and language programmes	• Work in partnership with other agencies such as FE colleges, youth service, social services, health services, housing, employers and training providers, voluntary organisations	• Provide observations on SEN pupils and feedback to teachers and TAs
• Involved in school-based attendance projects	• Contribute to whole-school in-service training on speech, language and communication difficulties	• Help young people to access volunteering, community activities or sport	• Advise on appropriate SEN resources for learning
• Provide consultation and advice to schools on attendance strategy and individual cases	• Advise on resources, ICT and communication aids	• Give talks and leading group discussions in schools	• Give demonstration lessons
• Liaise with Home Education and Out of School Learning Services	• Help teachers and TAs to differentiate the curriculum	• Help young people to overcome racial, gender, disability and other types of discrimination	• Advise on personalised learning approaches and curriculum modifications
• Monitor the licensing of child employment and child entertainment in the local area	• Liaise with parents/carers on how they can help to support and promote their child's speech, language and communication needs at home	• Work with parents and carers to enable them to support their child's career aspirations	• Contribute to whole-school staff in-service training
• Provide professional advice and support to schools and education staff on safeguarding arrangements, including child protection	• Monitor and evaluate the impact of speech and language programmes delivered to pupils	• Access community support from the arts, study support and other guidance networks in the local area, particularly in finding work experience placements	• Advise teachers/SENCOs on specific interventions and programmes for pupils with SEN
• Take a lead role in allegations against members of staff and volunteers	• Work collaboratively with other professionals such as the educational psychologist, school nurse, occupational therapist	• Keep in contact with the young people they work with, and monitor progress and outcomes	• Provide feedback on the progress of SEN/LDD pupils in their specific intervention programmes
• Provide training to schools, governors and education staff, e.g. INSET, coaching and mentoring			• Monitor and evaluate programmes and interventions being delivered
• Support and advise parents to ensure they fulfil their statutory responsibilities with respect to the education of their children			• Liaise with other practitioners and colleagues
• Involvement in any court action where parents/carers are being prosecuted for their child's non-attendance at school			• Liaise with the parents of SEN/LDD pupils and keep them informed of progress in intervention programmes
			• Advise on classroom management approaches for pupils with SEN

The role of the school improvement partner and SEN, disability and *ECM*

Every school and pupil referral unit (PRU) in England has a school improvement partner (SIP). The SIP is likely to be a current ex-headteacher, a local authority adviser or a school improvement officer. The SIP meets with the headteacher at least once every term to support and challenge him or her on how well the school/PRU is performing overall. In particular, the SIP will explore with the school/PRU:

- how it is analysing the impact of its actions on raising standards and improving the progress of all pupils;
- the accuracy of its self-evaluation in relation to making judgements about all aspects of its effectiveness;
- whether the school improvement priorities are appropriate, and the progress being made towards achieving them;
- identifying strengths and good practice which is worth disseminating;
- the benefits gained from its partnerships and additional support;
- what, if any, other support the school/PRU would benefit from;
- the effectiveness of leadership and management, including governance;
- the outcomes of the last Ofsted inspection, and progress towards addressing any areas for improvement arising from the inspection;
- the level of challenge in setting agreed statutory targets;
- the headteacher's performance management objectives, and new objectives for the next cycle of improvement.

While it is important for newly qualified teachers and TAs to know what the SIP will be focusing on with the headteacher, it is even more important that they are aware of what the SIP will be exploring in relation to SEN, disability and *ECM*, and how they are responding to the SIP's questions at classroom level.

SIP questions on SEN and disability

- Are the needs of pupils with SEN/LDD being met at classroom level?
- Is SEN support/provision well planned and co-ordinated?
- Do SEN/LDD pupils in your class have access to a broad, balanced, relevant and differentiated curriculum?
- Are SEN/LDD pupils in your class getting comparable access to extended services and extra-curricular activities to that of all other pupils?
- Are pupils with SEN/LDD in your class making sufficient progress in their learning and well-being, in relation to their prior attainment? Is this progress good enough, and if not, how are you narrowing the gaps in their attainment?
- Are there any particular cohorts of pupils with SEN/LDD in your class who are underachieving? If so, what are you doing to address this issue?
- What has been the impact of any additional interventions or catch-up programmes being delivered to pupils with SEN/LDD?

- Is the deployment of TAs and other additional supporting adults effective enough? If not, what will you do to improve their impact?

- How are you tracking and monitoring SEN/LDD pupil progress?

- What has been the attendance, punctuality, attitude and behaviour of pupils with SEN/LDD in your class? Are there any issues, and if so, what action is being taken to improve any or all of these aspects?

- What has been the impact of any SEN CPD you have attended over the last academic year, in relation to meeting the needs of SEN/LDD pupils?

SIP questions on *Every Child Matters*

- To what extent are *ECM* outcomes being included in teacher planning?

- How are you contributing to improving pupils' *ECM* outcomes?

- Are there any barriers to you meeting the *ECM* strategy?

- How are practitioners from the children's workforce in and outside the education setting improving SEN/LDD pupils' *ECM* well-being?

- How are you managing the *ECM* systems such as the CAF, TAC, ContactPoint, lead professional?

- How do you ensure the views of pupils with SEN/LDD are listened to and acted upon?

- How are SEN/LDD pupils in your class progressing in all of the five *ECM* outcomes: be healthy, stay safe, enjoy and achieve, make a positive contribution, achieve economic well-being?

- What has been the impact on your *ECM* practice of attending in-service training on *Every Child Matters* over the last academic year?

The role of the Advanced Skills Teacher/Excellent Teacher for SEN

The role of all ASTs is primarily to provide and drive forward excellent teaching and learning within their own and other schools. ASTs will also have strengths in a curriculum subject at primary or secondary phase, or they may have expertise in SEN and BESD, or they may be an AST for initial teacher training (ITT).

The ASTs' main duties, in relation to their area of expertise, are to:

- work with other teachers on classroom organisation and teaching methods, providing model lessons;

- help teachers to develop strategies for pupils experiencing difficulties or for the most able pupils;

- lead continuing professional development activities and deliver workshops or in-service training on aspects of teaching and learning;

- disseminate best practice in relation to inclusion, managing challenging behaviour, and tackling underachievement;

- produce high-quality teaching materials, promote the use of new technologies and help teachers update existing schemes of work;

- undertake lesson observations in other schools and provide feedback;
- mentor newly qualified and trainee teachers;
- provide exemplar lessons for trainee teachers;
- contribute to the assessment of trainee teachers and of student teaching practice.

Excellent Teachers focus on whole-school teaching and learning issues within their own school. They do not do any outreach work in other schools. They maintain the same class teaching responsibility as ASTs. The Excellent Teacher's main duties are to:

- achieve improvements in teaching and learning across their own school;
- participate in the induction of newly qualified teachers;
- participate in the professional mentoring of other teachers;
- deliver demonstration lessons to share good practice;
- help other teachers to develop their expertise in planning, preparation and assessment;
- help other teachers to evaluate the impact of their teaching on pupils;
- undertake classroom observations;
- help other teachers improve their teaching practice, particularly those who are on capability procedures.

The role of the local authority SEN and Inclusion Consultant

The local authority SEN and Inclusion Consultant's main role is to support teachers in meeting the legal requirements of the SEN Code of Practice, and to deliver the national strategies in relation to SEN and inclusion. They are usually seconded to the post, and are all experienced teachers with outstanding or good classroom practice. The SEN and Inclusion Consultant's main duties are to:

- provide training, consultancy and support for teachers' professional development in SEN and inclusion in primary and secondary schools;
- contribute to the development, monitoring and evaluation of SEN and inclusion provision within the local authority;
- support schools in including pupils with a diversity of SEN/LDD and AEN;
- provide support to the SENCO in relation to policy guidance and provision management and mapping;
- support the induction and training of newly appointed and experienced SENCOs and NQTs in relation to SEN, disability and inclusion;
- organise and run the termly LA SENCO networks, as well as contribute to the NQT networks when SEND and inclusion are a focus.

Useful resources to support collaborative work with other practitioners

The following resources relating to work with other practitioners will provide a valuable point of reference to trainee and newly qualified teachers/TAs.

Web-based resources

Two useful government parent websites offer helpful information: http//www.parents centre.gov.uk/; and http//www.everychildmatters.gov.uk/parents/parentsknowhow/

Working with Parents – Primary – Involving Parents is a Teachers TV video at http://www.teachers.tv/video/2851

Secondary Parents and Community Videos on Teachers TV website are at http://teachers.tv/video/browser/811/1081

Working with Other Adults in the Class is taken from the TTRB online resource called *SEN A Guide*, which can be accessed at http//www.sen.ttrb.ac.uk/

Secondary Support Staff – Multi-agency Working is a Teachers TV video that looks at the work of an in-house multi-agency support team working in an inner–city secondary school: http//www.teachers.tv/video/3407

School Matters – Every Child Matters and Multi-agency Working is a Teachers TV video which exemplifies different approaches to working with pupil support agencies: http://www.teachers.tv/video/22456/resources

What multi–agency working means for a range of practitioners working in schools is covered in http://www.everychildmatters.gov.uk/deliveringservices/multiagency working/workingwithothers/whatitmeansforme/

Useful publications by Rita Cheminais

Effective Multi-agency Partnerships. Putting Every Child Matters into Practice (2009) London: SAGE Publications.

Every Child Matters: A Practical Guide for Teachers (2006) London: David Fulton

Every Child Matters: A Practical Guide for Teaching Assistants (2008) Abingdon: Routledge

Questions for reflection

1 What aspects of partnership with TAs/LSAs do you want to improve, and how will you go about doing this?

2 What have been your experiences of working with other multi-agency practitioners in your classroom/education setting?

3 What have been the benefits of working with practitioners from other services for you and your pupils with additional needs?

4 Which one aspect of multi-agency partnership work have you found most problematic, and how could it be improved?

5 What has been your involvement with CAF, TAC, ContactPoint or the lead professional, and how have any or all of these systems and procedures enabled you to understand collaborative work better?

6 Having spent time with the SENCO in your setting, what has been the most valuable advice and support you have gained from him/her, and what other advice and support would you welcome in relation to SEN and disability?

7 What progress have you made towards meeting the relevant professional standards for collaborative work and the GTC Joint Statement for Inter-professional Working?

8 How useful have you found knowing what the school improvement partner's focus will be in relation to SEND and *ECM*, and how has it helped you to have a greater focus on the impact of multi-agency collaborative work on outcomes for your pupils?

9 How far do you consider the enhanced focus on pupil well-being is compromising teachers'/TAs' work in teaching and learning?

10 'Teachers are expected to be social workers now with the *ECM* agenda.' How far do you agree or disagree with this statement?

11 How will reading this chapter influence or change your practice in relation to working with other practitioners/colleagues?

Glossary

Accelerated learning covers the range of practical approaches that enable pupils to learn how to learn. It includes using approaches such as mind maps, multiple intelligences, multi-sensory learning approaches and thinking skills.

Achievement describes the pupils' knowledge, skills and understanding gained through the subjects of the curriculum, and the attitudes, values and other aspects of personal development fostered by the school and developed within and beyond the formal curriculum.

Assessing pupil progress is a systematic approach to periodic assessment that provides teachers with diagnostic information about individual pupil progress, which is based on a range of evidence.

Assessment for learning is the process of identifying pupils' learning needs; of seeking and interpreting evidence for use by pupils, teachers and other professionals to decide where the pupils are in their learning; what they need to do to improve and how to get there.

Assistive technology is any item, piece of equipment or product system that is used to improve functional capabilities of individuals with disabilities.

Attention Deficit Hyperactivity Disorder is an inherited condition, more prevalent among boys than among girls, which results in inattention, impulsiveness, hyperactivity and day dreaming.

Autistic spectrum disorder is the condition of pupils who find it difficult to understand and use non-verbal and verbal communication and social behaviour or to think and behave flexibly.

Behavioural, emotional and social difficulty is behaviour that presents a barrier to learning, and which persists in some pupils despite teachers using and following the school's behaviour policy and procedures. Pupils with BESD may become isolated, withdrawn, disruptive or hyperactive, lack concentration, have immature social skills or present challenging behaviours.

Bullying is any behaviour by an individual or group of pupils which is repeated over time that intentionally hurts another pupil or group of pupils either physically or emotionally. Bullying usually involves verbal taunts, name calling, physical injury, damage to property, rumour spreading, ridicule or shunning.

Collaboration is the process of working jointly with others to develop and achieve common goals.

Colleagues are all those professionals with whom a teacher may have a professional relationship. They include other teachers, teaching assistants and learning mentors as well as those in the wider workforce of social care, health and education.

Common Assessment Framework is a holistic assessment process used by professionals and practitioners in the children's workforce to assess the additional needs of children and young people at the first sign of difficulty.

Community cohesion refers to the process of working towards a harmonious society which values diversity and offers equal opportunities for all. Schools, along with the workplace and the wider community, contribute to building community cohesion with strong and positive relationships between individuals.

ContactPoint is a quick way of finding out which other practitioners from external agencies are working with the same child or young person.

Contextual value added compares the progress made by each pupil with the average progress made by similar pupils in similar schools.

Deep learning is achieved by pupils who are articulate, autonomous and collaborative learners, and who reflect on their learning. Deep learning is secured through pupil voice, assessment for learning and learning to learn.

Disabled describes the condition of any individual who has a physical or mental impairment which has a substantial and long-term adverse effect on their ability to carry out normal day-to-day activities. The term also covers those with sensory or intellectual impairments, those with a learning disability or those who are incontinent, have AIDS, severe disfigurements or progressive conditions such as muscular dystrophy.

Dual or multiple exceptionalities are characteristic of those pupils who both have special educational needs and also are gifted or talented. They are highly able but the special educational need hinders the effective expression of their high ability.

Dual placement refers to a special school pupil who attends a mainstream school for 51 per cent or more of their time.

Dyscalculia is the condition of pupils who have difficulty in acquiring mathematical skills. These pupils have difficulty understanding simple number concepts and have problems learning number facts and procedures.

Dyslexia is the condition of pupils who have a marked and persistent difficulty in learning to read, write and spell, despite making progress in other subject areas. Dyslexic pupils tend to have poor memories, poor reading comprehension skills, and poor handwriting and punctuation skills. They also experience difficulties in concentration, organisation and remembering sequences of words. They may also reverse letters or sounds in words.

Dyspraxia affects pupils who experience difficulties in the organisation of movement, often making them appear to be clumsy. They struggle with tasks that require manual dexterity. They also have poor balance, and therefore find running, skipping, hopping, holding a pencil or doing jigsaws difficult.

Emotional intelligence is the ability to develop emotional sensitivity as well as the capacity to learn healthy emotional management skills.

Emotional literacy means managing one's own emotions, and being able to understand the feelings of others.

Evaluation means judging the quality, effectiveness, strengths and weaknesses of provision, based on robust evidence collected during review and monitoring processes.

Extended school is one that provides a range of services and activities, often beyond the school day, to help meet the needs of its pupils, their families and the wider community.

Formative assessment is the ongoing assessment at regular intervals of a pupil's progress with accompanying feedback to help them improve further.

Group education plan is utilised where a small group of SEN pupils share similar learning difficulties in a class. Although there is one plan for the group of pupils, the assessment of whether pupils have achieved the targets set must be made on an individual pupil basis.

Guided learning is an arrangement whereby a small group of no more than six pupils work in the mainstream classroom on consolidating and applying their learning when undertaking tailored and focused work which is reviewed with the teacher or TA.

Hearing impairment ranges from a mild, moderate or severe hearing loss to profound deafness. HI pupils cover the whole ability range. Pupils with HI usually have to use a hearing aid, and have adaptations made to their environment and teaching. Some of these pupils will communicate through signing.

Inclusion is concerned with promoting the belonging, presence, participation and achievement of the full diversity of children and young people. It is an ongoing process, focused on how children and young people are helped to learn, achieve and participate fully in the activities and life of the school and the community. It is also a process of identifying, understanding and breaking down barriers to participation.

Individual education plan is a teaching and planning tool with three or four short-term targets, appropriate strategies and a record of the outcomes for individual SEN pupils in Action or Action Plus and with a statement of SEN.

Information sharing is the passing on of relevant information to other agencies, organisations and individuals that require it in order to deliver better services to children and young people.

Lead professional is a designated professional from health, social services or education who has regular contact with a child or young person with SEN. They co-ordinate and monitor service provision, acting as a gatekeeper for information sharing.

Learning difficulties and/or disabilities are characteristic of pupils who have difficulty in acquiring new skills or who learn at a different rate from their peers. It includes pupils with disabilities defined in the Disability Discrimination Act 2001. The term is used across education, health and social services in relation to children and young people aged 0 to 19.

Looked after children are any children or young people in the care of the local authority or provided with accommodation by the LA social services department for a continuous period of more than twenty-four hours.

Moderate learning difficulties are the difficulties of those pupils whose attainments are well below expected levels in all or most areas of the curriculum, despite appropriate interventions. They have difficulty in acquiring basic literacy and numeracy skills and in understanding concepts. They may also have speech and language delay, low self-esteem, low levels of concentration and underdeveloped social skills.

Monitoring is the systematic checking on progress and the gathering of information to establish the extent to which agreed plans, policies, statutory requirements or intervention programmes and strategies are being implemented.

Multi-sensory impairment is the condition of pupils who have a combination of visual and hearing difficulties, sometimes referred to as deaf blind pupils. They have greater difficulty accessing the curriculum and the learning environment than those with a single sensory impairment. They also have difficulty with perception, communication and the acquisition of information.

National Service Framework provides a set of quality standards for health, social care and some education services, and is aimed at reducing inequalities in service provision, in order to improve the lives and health of children and young people.

Pedagogy is the act of teaching and the rationale that supports the actions that teachers take. It includes what a teacher needs to know and the range of skills that he/she needs to use in order to make effective teaching decisions.

Personalised learning is the process of tailoring and matching teaching and learning around the way different pupils learn in order to meet their individual needs, interests and aptitudes and enable them to reach their optimum potential.

Physical disability affects those pupils who require significant adaptations to enable them to access the curriculum. It also refers to those with mild PD who are able to learn effectively without additional provision. Some may have SEN, a sensory impairment, a learning difficulty or neurological problems. The physical disability may impact on a pupil's mobility. Examples of PD are: cerebral palsy, heart disease, spina bifida, hydrocephalus, muscular dystrophy.

Practitioner is the generic term used to refer to those who work directly with children and young people in a range of settings, including schools and early years settings.

Profound and multiple learning difficulties are characteristic of those pupils who have complex and severe learning difficulties and who are likely to be educated in special schools. They are likely to have physical disabilities, a sensory impairment or a severe medical condition. PMLD pupils require a high level of adult support for their learning and personal care. Their attainment is usually below NC level 1, and in the early P scale range of P1 to P4.

Quality-first teaching is the daily repertoire of teaching strategies and techniques used for all pupils in the mainstream classroom that ensures pupils' progression in learning.

RAISEonline is a web-based system which contains data about a school's basic characteristics, attainment and progress in the core subjects, to support evaluation and target setting.

Review is a retrospective activity which collects and assesses a wide range of information including perceptions, opinions and judgements relating to a particular intervention programme, additional provision or initiative.

Safeguarding describes the process of identifying children and young people who have suffered or are likely to suffer significant harm, and taking the appropriate action to keep them safe.

Self-esteem is the way individuals see, think and feel about themselves. It also relates to how individuals judge their self-worth, as well as how they think others perceive them and feel about them.

Self-evaluation is the ongoing, formative, rigorous evidence-gathering process, embedded in the daily work of the classroom and school, which gives an honest assessment of their strengths, weaknesses and effectiveness.

Severe learning difficulties affect those pupils who have significant intellecttual or cognitive impairments which have a major impact on their ability to participate in the school curriculum without support. They may have accompanying difficulties in co-ordination, communication and perception, as well as in acquiring self-help skills. SLD pupils are likely to be functioning on the P scales or at the lower levels of the NC.

Social and emotional aspects of learning (SEAL) is a national whole-school strategy that helps to promote the social and emotional aspects of pupils' learning, i.e. self-awareness, managing feelings, motivation, empathy and social skills. It is a programme used in the primary and secondary phases of education.

Speech and language and communication needs (SLCN) are the needs of those pupils who have difficulty in understanding information and/or in making others understand them. They are usually significantly behind their peers in the acquisition of speech and oral language skills. Their speech may be poor or unintelligible and they may use words inappropriately or incorrectly.

Summative assessment is the summary of pupils' overall learning or final achievement at the end of an academic year, or at the end of a course of study. It may also involve pupils in undertaking a standardised test or external examination or being subject to teacher assessment.

Teaching repertoire describes the set of skills and techniques that engage pupils' active participation in learning. These include generic skills such as questioning, explaining, guiding and organising group work.

Team around the child is an individualised, personalised and evolving team of a few different practitioners who come together to provide practical support to help an individual child or young person.

Transfer refers to the move from one school or phase of education to another.

Transition refers to the move from one year group to the next within the same school or education setting.

Visual impairment describes a range of difficulties from partial sight through to total blindness, requiring that adaptations be made to the environment as well as specific differentiation of learning materials to access the curriculum.

Vulnerable children are those children at risk of social exclusion, those who are disadvantaged and those whose life chances are likely to be jeopardised unless more action is taken to meet their needs.

Well-being refers to the five *Every Child Matters* outcomes. It also means having the basic things needed to live, be healthy and stay safe.

References and further reading

Assessment Reform Group (2002) *Assessment for Learning: 10 Principles. Research-Based Principles to Guide Classroom Practice*. London: Institute of Education, University of London

Audit Commission (2002) *Special Educational Needs: a Mainstream Issue*. London: Audit Commission

Becta (2007) *Making Software Accessible. A Guide for Schools*. Coventry: British Educational Communications and Technology Agency

Behaviour4Learning (2008) *A Set of 20 Scenarios for Tutors, School Mentors and Trainee Teachers*, http://www.behaviour4 learning.ac.uk, accessed 22 November 2008

Briggs, S. (2004) *Inclusion and How to Do It. Meeting SEN in Secondary Classrooms*. London: David Fulton

Briggs, S. (2005) *Inclusion and How to Do It. Meeting SEN in Primary Classrooms*. London: David Fulton

Buttriss, J. and Callander, A. (2003) *A–Z of Special Needs for Every Teacher*. London: pfp

Cheminais, R. (2004) *How to Create the Inclusive Classroom. Removing Barriers to Learning*. London: David Fulton

Cheminais, R. (2006) *Every Child Matters. A Practical Guide for Teachers*. London: David Fulton

Cheminais, R. (2008) *Every Child Matters. A Practical Guide for Teaching Assistants*. Abingdon: Routledge

Cheminais, R. (2009) *Effective Multi-Agency Partnerships. Putting Every Child Matters into Practice*. London: Sage Publications

Cheminais, R. (2009) *The Pocket Guide to Every Child Matters*. Abingdon: Routledge

CWDC (2008a) *The Common Assessment Framework and Schools Fact Sheet*. London: Children's Workforce Development Council

CWDC (2008b) *Common Assessment Framework for Children and Young People (CAF). CAF Form*. London: Children's Workforce Development Council

Daniels, H. and Porter, J. (2007) *Learning Needs and Difficulties Among Children of Primary School Age: Definition, Identification, Provision and Issues*. Primary Review Research Briefing 5/2. Cambridge: University of Cambridge

DCSF (2007a) *The SEN Statutory Framework*, http://www.standards.dfes.gov.uk/primary/features/inclusion/sen/idp, accessed 11 November 2008

DCSF (2007b) *Advanced Skills Teachers. Promoting Excellence*. Nottingham: Department for Children, Schools and Families

DCSF (2007c) *Excellent Teachers. Guidance for Teachers, Headteachers and Local Authorities (England)*. Nottingham: Department for Children, Schools and Families

DCSF (2008a) *Gifted and Talented Education: Helping to Find and Support Children with Dual or Multiple Exceptionalities*. Nottingham: Department for Children, Schools and Families

DCSF (2008b) *Personalised Learning – A Practical Guide*. Nottingham: Department for Children, Schools and Families

DCSF (2008c) *Bullying Involving Children with Special Educational Needs and Disabilities. Safe to Learn: Embedding Anti-bullying Work in Schools*. Nottingham: Department for Children, Schools and Families

DCSF (2008d) *Information Sharing: Pocket Guide*. Nottingham: Department for Children, Schools and Families

DCSF (2008e) *The Education of Children and Young People with Behavioural, Emotional and Social Difficulties as a Special Educational Need*. Nottingham: Department for Children, Schools and Families

DCSF (2008f) *Inclusion Development Programme. Supporting Children with Speech, Language and Communication Needs: Guidance for Practitioners in the Early Years Foundation Stage*. Nottingham: Department for Children, Schools and Families

DCSF (2008g) *Inclusion Development Programme Primary/Secondary Dyslexia and Speech, Language and Communication Needs. An Interactive Resource to Support Headteachers, Leadership Teams, Teachers and Support Staff*. Nottingham: Department for Children, Schools and Families

DCSF (2008h) *Initial Teacher Training Inclusion Development Programme Primary/Secondary. Dyslexia and Speech, Language and Communication Needs. An Interactive Resource to Support Initial Teacher Training Institutions and Trainee Teachers.* Nottingham: Department for Children, Schools and Families

DfEE (1996) *The Education Act.* London: Her Majesty's Stationery Office

DfEE (1997) *Excellence for All Children: Meeting Special Educational Needs.* London: Department for Education and Employment

DfEE (1998) *Meeting Special Educational Needs. A Programme of Action.* Suffolk: Department for Education and Employment

DfEE (1999a) *Social Inclusion: Pupil Support* (Circular 10/99). London: Department for Education and Employment

DfEE (1999b) *Social Inclusion: The LEA Role in Pupil Support* (Circular 11/99). London: Department for Education and Employment

DfEE (2001a) *Promoting Children's Mental Health within Early Years and School Settings.* Nottingham: Department for Education and Employment

DfEE (2001b) *Supporting the Target Setting Process. Guidance for Effective Target Setting for Pupils with Special Educational Needs* (revised March 2001). Nottingham: Department for Education and Employment and Qualifications and Curriculum Authority

DfEE/QCA (1998) *Supporting the Target Setting Process. Guidance for Effective Target Setting for Pupils with Special Educational Needs.* Nottingham: Department for Education and Employment and Qualifications and Curriculum Authority

DfEE/QCA (1999a) *The National Curriculum. Handbook for Primary Teachers in England.* London: Department for Education and Employment and the Qualifications and Curriculum Authority

DfEE/QCA (1999b) *The National Curriculum. Handbook for Secondary Teachers in England.* London: Department for Education and Employment and the Qualifications and Curriculum Authority

DfES (2001a) *Inclusive Schooling: Children with Special Educational Needs.* London: Department for Education and Skills

DfES (2001b) *Special Educational Needs and Disability Act.* London: The Stationery Office

DfES (2001c) *Special Educational Needs Code of Practice.* London: Department for Education and Skills

DfES (2001d) *SEN Toolkit.* London: Department for Education and Skills

DfES (2002) *Accessible Schools: Summary Guidance.* London: Department for Education and Skills

DfES (2003a) *Every Child Matters.* London: Department for Education and Skills

DfES (2003b) *What to Do if You're Worried a Child is Being Abused. Summary.* London: Department for Education and Skills

DfES (2003c) *The Report of the Special Schools Working Group.* Nottingham: Department for Education and Skills

DfES (2004a) *Teaching Strategies and Approaches for Pupils with Special Educational Needs: A Scoping Study.* RR516. Nottingham: Department for Education and Skills

DfES (2004b) *Removing Barriers to Achievement. The Government's Strategy for SEN.* Nottingham: Department for Education and Skills

DfES (2004c) *Safeguarding Children in Education.* London: Department for Education and Skills

DfES (2004d) *Every Child Matters: Change for Children in Schools.* London: Department for Education and Skills

DfES (2004e) *The Children Act.* Norwich: Her Majesty's Stationery Office

DfES (2004f) *Learning and Teaching for Children with Special Educational Needs in the Primary Years.* Nottingham: Department for Education and Skills

DfES (2004g) *Every Child Matters: Next Steps.* Nottingham: Department for Education and Skills

DfES (2005a) *Leading on Inclusion.* Norwich: Department for Education and Skills

DfES (2005b) *Data Collection by Type of Special Educational Need.* Nottingam: Department for Education and Skills

DfES (2005c) *Promoting Inclusion and Tackling Underperformance. Maximising Progress: Ensuring the Attainment of Pupils with SEN. Part 2: Approaches to Learning and Teaching in the Classroom.* Norwich: Department for Education and Skills

DfES (2005d) *Secondary National Strategy. Tracking for Success.* Norwich: Department for Education and Skills

DfES (2005e) *Special Educational Needs and Disability Update 18.* Sudbury: Department for Education and Skills

DfES (2006a) *Implementing the Disability Discrimination Act in Schools and Early Years Settings.* London: Department for Education and Skills

DfES (2006b) *Common Assessment Framework for Children and Young People. Practitioners' Guide.* Nottingham: Department for Education and Skills

DfES (2006c) *Common Assessment Framework for Children and Young People (CAF). Pre-assessment Checklist.* London: Department for Education and Skills

DfES (2006d) *Promoting the Disability Equality Duty.* London: Department for Education and Skills

DfES (2006e) *What to Do if You're Worried a Child is Being Abused – Summary*. Nottingham: Department for Education and Skills

DfES (2007a) *Gifted and Talented Education. Guidance on Preventing Underachievement: A Focus on Dual or Multiple Exceptionality (DME)*. Norwich: Department for Education and Skills

DfES (2007b) *Pedagogy and Personalisation*. Norwich: Department for Education and Skills

DfES (2007c) *Implementing the Disability Discrimination Act in Schools and Early Years Settings. A Training Resource for Schools and Local Authorities*. Wetherby: The Stationery Office

DH/DfES (2004a) *National Service Framework for Children, Young People and Maternity Services. Executive Summary*. London: Department of Health/Department for Education and Skills

DH/DfES (2004b) *Promoting Emotional Health and Well Being Through the National Healthy School Standard*. Wetherby: Health Development Agency, Department of Health/Department for Education and Skills

DRC (1995) *Disability Discrimination Act*. London: Her Majesty's Stationery Office

DRC (2002a) *Code of Practice for Schools: Disability Discrimination Act 1995, Part 4*. London: The Stationery Office and the Disability Rights Commission

DRC (2005) *The Disability Discrimination Act*. London: Disability Rights Commission

Dyson, A., Farrell, P., Hutcheson, G., Polat, F. and Gallannaugh, F. (2004) *Inclusion and Pupil Achievement*. Nottingham: Department for Education and Skills

East, V. and Evans, L. (2006) *At a Glance. A Practical Guide to Children's Special Needs*. London: Continuum

Ellis, S., Tod, J. and Graham-Matheson, L. (2008) *Special Educational Needs and Inclusion: Reflection and Renewal*. Birmingham: NASUWT

GTC (2007a) *Inter-professional Values Underpinning Work with Children and Young People. Joint Statement*. London: General Teaching Council for England

GTC (2007b) *Making SENse of CPD. A GTC Resource File on Professional Education and Development for Teachers in Relation to Special Educational Needs (SEN)*, http://www.gtce.org.uk/networks/connect/resources/sen/, accessed 2 November 2008

GTC (2007c) *A Resource File for New Teachers: Special Educational Needs (SEN)*, http://www.gtce.org.uk/networks/engagehome/resources/sen_spring07, accessed 13 December 2008

Hook, P. and Vass, A. (2000) *Confident Classroom Leadership*. London: David Fulton

Hull Learning Services (2005) *Supporting Children with Behaviour Difficulties*. London: David Fulton

Hurst, T. (2004) *Meeting SEN in the Curriculum: English*. London: David Fulton

Key, T. (2009) 'A Third of Schools Bore their Classes', *Times Educational Supplement* 9 January, p.12

Kirby, A. (2006) *Mapping SEN. Routes through Identification to Intervention*. Abingdon: Routledge/David Fulton

Leslie, C. and Skidmore, C. (2007) *SEN: The Truth about Inclusion*. London: The Bow Group

Long, R. (1999) *Developing Self-esteem through Positive Entrapment for Pupils Facing Emotional and Behavioural Difficulties*. Tamworth: NASEN

Ofsted (2000) *Evaluating Educational Inclusion*. London: Office for Standards in Education

Ofsted (2004) *Special Educational Needs and Disability. Towards Inclusive Schools*. London: Office for Standards in Education

Ofsted (2005) *Removing Barriers: a 'Can-do' Attitude. A Report on Developing Good Practice for Children with Special Needs in Early Years Childcare and Education in the Private and Voluntary Sectors* (HMI 2449). London: Office for Standards in Education

Ofsted (2006a) *Inclusion: Does it Matter Where Pupils Are Taught? Provision and Outcomes in Different Settings for Pupils with Learning Difficulties and Disabilities*. London: Office for Standards in Education

Ofsted (2006b) *Improving Performance through School Self-evaluation and Improvement Planning: Further Guidance*. London: Office for Standards in Education

Ofsted (2008a) *Indicators of a School's Contribution to Well Being. Consultation Document*. London: Office for Standards in Education, Children's Services and Skills

Ofsted (2008b) *A Focus on Improvement. An Evaluation Report: Responses to Ofsted's Consultation on Proposed Changes to Maintained School Inspections*. London: Office for Standards in Education, Children's Services and Skills

Ofsted (2008c) *How Well New Teachers Are Prepared to Teach Pupils with Learning Difficulties and/or Disabilities*. London: Office for Standards in Education, Children's Services and Skills

Ofsted (2008d) *Using the Evaluation Schedule. Guidance for Inspectors of Schools*. London: Office for Standards in Education, Children's Services and Skills

Ofsted (2008e) *A Focus on Improvement: Proposals for Maintained School Inspections from September 2009*. London: Office for Standards in Education, Children's Services and Skills

QCA (2001a) *Supporting School Improvement. Emotional and Behavioural Development.* London: Qualifications and Curriculum Authority

QCA (2001b) *Planning, Teaching and Assessing the Curriculum for Pupils with Learning Difficulties.* London: Qualifications and Curriculum Authority

QCA (2005) *Using the P Scales. Assessing, Moderating and Reporting Pupil Attainment in English, Mathematics and Science at Levels P4 to P8.* Norwich: Qualifications and Curriculum Authority

QCA (2008) *Every Child Matters at the heart of the curriculum.* London: Qualifications and Curriculum Authority

Seba, J. *et al.* (2007) *An Investigation of Personalised Learning Approaches Used by Schools.* Nottingham: Department for Education and Skills

Spohrer, K. (2002) *Supporting Children with Attention Deficit Hyperactive Disorder.* Birmingham: Questions Publishing

TDA (2006) *Special Educational Needs in Mainstream Schools. A Guide for the Beginner Teacher.* London: Training and Development Agency for Schools

TDA (2007a) *Professional Standards for Teachers. Qualified Teacher Status.* London: Training and Development Agency for Schools

TDA (2007b) *Supporting the Induction Process. TDA Guidance for Newly Qualified Teachers.* London: Training and Development Agency for Schools

TDA (2007c) *National Occupational Standards for Supporting Teaching and Learning in Schools: Unit Titles and their Elements.* London: Training and Development Agency for Schools

TDA (2007d) *What is Every Child Matters?* London: Training and Development Agency for Schools

Teaching and Learning in 2020 Review Group (2006) *2020 Vision: Report of the Teaching and Learning in 2020 Review Group.* London: Department for Education and Skills

TSO (2006a) *House of Commons Education and Skills Committee. Special Educational Needs. Third Report of Session 2005–2006. Volume 1.* London: The Stationery Office

TSO (2006b) *Government Response to the Education and Skills Committee Report on Special Educational Needs (October 2006).* Norwich: The Stationery Office.

TTRB (2008) *Special Educational Needs and/or Disabilities: Undergraduate Primary Materials for ITE,* http://www.sen.ttrb.ac.uk/, accessed 22 November 2008

Warnock, M. (1978) *Report of the Committee of Inquiry into the Education of Handicapped Children and Young People.* London: Her Majesty's Stationery Office

Warnock, M. (2005) *Special Educational Needs: A New Look. Paper 11.* London: Philosophy of Education Society of Great Britain

Wilmot, E. (2006) *Personalising Learning in the Primary Classroom. A Practical Guide for Teachers and School Leaders.* Carmarthen: Crown House Publishing

Index